"Through the Valley . . ."

"Through the Valley..."
Prayers for Violent Times

Margaret Anne Huffman

. . . though I walk through the valley of the shadow . . .
Psalm 23

Judson Press ® Valley Forge

"Through the Valley . . . ": Prayers for Violent Times
© 1996, Judson Press, Valley Forge, PA 19482-0851

Bible quotations marked GNB in this volume are from the *Good News Bible,* the Bible in Today's English Version. Copyright © American Bible Society, 1976. Used by permission. Bible quotations marked KJV in this volume are from *The Holy Bible,* King James Version. Bible quotations marked NASB in this volume are from the New American Standard Bible, © 1960, 1962, 1963, 1968, 1971, 1972, 1973, 1975, 1977 by The Lockman Foundation. Used by permission. Bible quotations marked NIV in this volume are from HOLY BIBLE: *New International Version,* copyright © 1973, 1978, 1984. Used by permission of Zondervan Bible Publishers. Bible quotations marked NKJV in this volume are from HOLY BIBLE, The New King James Version. Copyright © 1972, 1984 by Thomas Nelson Inc. Bible quotations marked RSV in this volume are from the Revised Standard Version of the Bible, copyright © 1946, 1952, 1971, by the Division of Christian Education of the National Council of the Churches of Christ in the U. S. A. Used by permission. Bible quotations marked TLB in this volume are from *The Living Bible,* copyright © 1971. Used by permission of Tyndale House Publishers, Inc., Wheaton, IL 60189. All rights reserved.

Library of Congress Cataloging-in-Publication Data
Huffman, Margaret Anne.
    "Through the valley—" : prayers for violent times / Margaret Anne Huffman.
      p. cm.
      ISBN 0-8170-1238-9 (pbk. : alk. paper)
    1. Consolation—Prayer-books and devotions—English. 2. Violence—Religious aspects—Christianity—Prayer-books and devotions—English. 3. Spiritual healing—Prayer-books and devotions—English. I. Title.
BV4909.H75 1996
242'.4—dc20
                                                      95-50509

Printed in the U.S.A.
05 04 03 02 01 00 99 98 97 96
10 9 8 7 6 5 4 3 2 1

Dedication

For **Gary**,
pathfinder and companion on a journey he made possible,
"This is my beloved, and this is my friend . . ."
(Song of Solomon 5:16 KJV)

AND

Lynn, Rob, Beth, who provide its continuing joy,
now overflowing through
Aaron and **Kali,** to begin with,
and **Jack** who showed me I could paddle up it

Contents

Preface

"Open my eyes to see wonderful things . . ."

"You need not fear any dangers at night or sudden attacks during the day . . ."

". . . though I walk through the valley . . ."

(Psalm 119:18, TLB; Psalm 91:5, GNB; Psalm 23:4, RSV)

Ah, sunny, carefree days of innocence and ease. But now they are past days—for *zing*, lightning bolts of violence are plunging us into darkness. Adult or child, victim or bystander, or simply touched by the mood of violence, we stumble in the dark, tripping over fear, anger. Adversaries over any issue—even peace—we reject negotiation, find despair and cynicism increasingly sweet, retaliation necessary, and faith as faint as a dwindling flashlight battery.

We feel like powerless prey in paths of marauding storms.

We need a new way to look *through* the dark valleys of violence, for we are not promised no valleys; instead, as the psalmist says, we are assured passage through. We need a way to live beyond hand wringing, finger pointing, and wrenching statistics: hate crimes growing; a kid abused every thirteen seconds; elderly women, kids under four at greatest risk of murder; one in three girls, one in six boys sexually abused; children as killers; nearly half of women who are murdered die at the hand of husband/boyfriend; in the time it takes to read this, one woman will have been raped. We can't bear to continue the laundry list of violent deeds, even as we're preoccupied with it.

Yet through the bleakest darkness, like fireflies blinking, blinking in a dark sky, shines that tantalizing lure of peace, forgiveness, and rekindled trust; these prayers can lead us there. Collected, like fireflies in a jar, they are gleaned from my years as a reporter covering violence/abuse issues, a member of Shelby County Child Protection Team, a minister's wife, a friend and relative, and from faltering moments in my own dark.

May they meet us *wherever* violence overtakes us and show that:

- God is already there, grieving first, assuring us that no word or feeling is unacceptable or unwelcome;
- others share our pain, show us options, guide recovery;
- forgiveness can free a surprising captive—us;
- healing follows a journey we build dot-to-dot *through* the darkness;
- we resume lives in a world of good *and* evil, light *and* dark, cautious, but not hostages to fear.

Like captured fireflies set free from a jar to fly again against the dark sky, God's presence helps us repair and redeem violated bodies, minds, souls. In grace, we are passing through, not camping in, dark valleys.

I am grateful to those who shared the light they used, inspiring my words: abused, recovering children and their drawings, their resiliency; violated adults and their testimonies, their steadfast family members, their friends; advocates, guardians ad litem, caseworkers, counselors; John R. Hayes, M.D.; the Rev. Gary Huffman; the Rev. J. Lynn James; the Rev. Dr. Jack E. Skiles; Patricia Meyer; Mike Phillips; Mike, Dana, Marilyn, Susan at Gallahue; June, Shoshanna, staff; and especially the victims who became victors through telling their tales and reclaiming God's gift of wholeness.

Introduction

Fireflies on a Dark Sky

In a deadly random swipe, a spring storm tumbled people from their homes, dropped roofs on unwary sleepers, and when it reached our yard, felled a seventy-five-foot maple tree with lightning like a laser saw. We heard it crack, hesitate, go down. Had it missed the neighbors? the car? Abigail Old Cat? Captives to the night, power out, we hovered in the dark. Even after the storm whirled on east and we ventured to the porch, my eyes retained the afterimage of lightning. Eyes shut, I couldn't see beyond its repeated flash against my lids.

Reluctantly I finally opened my eyes. A spark. Neighbor's flashlight? Too small. Yet in the glow of that tiny flicker, I let out breath I'd been holding, unclenched my jaw. Another blink, another, another. Rain-soaked night is not fearsome darkness when fireflies come to call, their flickers replacing lightning's vivid marks on the eyes of our souls.

Violence, like lightning that topples trees and literally burns our eyes, stays with us. We sleep with lamps on and pray with one ear cocked. We become hostages to fear of violence recalled and dreaded: A car backfires; we hit the floor. Teens rush up behind us; we hug the wall, heart pounding. A car creeps on our bumper; we look for escape routes. A stranger stops; we run. Storms rumble; we close our eyes, hide.

Whether or not we are personally victimized, we become victims by association as others fall prey. We grieve for their pain in the same breath as we pray to be spared a similar fate. We feel abandoned by leaders, for the mood of violence spread from public office to pulpit to sensational talk shows creates a lush seedbed from which violent acts grow, frightening us more. We feel abandoned by a God who could intervene, protect, but doesn't.

Frantic and angry, we set alarms, bolt doors, buy guard dogs, and memorize where to hit, gouge, and kick, should dreaded become actual. We opt for simple solutions, knee-jerk reactions, and backlash. Fear paralyzes and vigilance exhausts, for there are no lightning rods to protect in these dark nights. Yet if we close our eyes in the dark and focus solely on zigzag bolts of trouble burned in afterimage, we miss the fireflies of hope.

Is there, we pray, *a future for peace? Is there reason for hope?*

To reach it, God of pilgrims and searchers, guard us from corrosive cynicism, despair, and hair-trigger tempers; restrain our urge to repay violence even with legal violence. We, your squabbling children, have dug ourselves a deep, dark hole no natural storm could match.

Even as we cower in the darkness, we feel God leading us through it to follow the blinking, blinking of fireflies. Their reminder of the natural order of healing is what we need to begin our journey toward it and away from violence's isolation. As the afterimage of lightning burned on the retina is healed by cells' chemical restoration, so, too, can our souls and bodies be healed by God's redeeming power of recovery, resiliency, comfort. With the psalmist we call from the dark, "Open my eyes to see wonderful things . . ." (Psalm 119:18, TLB).

And what of night's disasters? the illusions and assumptions that violence sends tumbling down like trees in the dark? Guided by God's presence in our violations and recoveries, may we be inspired to split logs and stack woodpiles of fallen trees to warm winter evenings on a blazing hearth. Hearing the fire's crackling energy, feeling its warmth on our backs when we edge up to it, breathing its dusky aroma, and dusting ashes from our hands, we will remember God's redeeming power, firefly bright.

Words of Light

The light shines in the darkness, and the darkness has not overcome it. (John 1:5, RSV)

Imitation Faith

You are either real or you aren't, O God of promises and covenants, and we need to find out right now. Evil's disasters are squeezing life from us. Vile, violent acts mock a faith we suddenly worry is good only for Sundays and sunshine. We are ill-equipped for the darkness outside our small circle of certainty. We confess, too, that we have worn our faith like a rabbit's foot on a key chain: If we kept it with us, nothing bad could befall us. Wrong, Lord, wrong, for darkness tarnishes lucky charms and saps imitation strength.

Help us to develop a street theology, for that is where we live. What happens here is different from what happens in the stained-glass vaults of safety, Lord of pageants and pretty Sunday-school pictures colored in rainbow crayons. No matter how upscale or downtrodden our own street may be, darkness stalks and doubt nips our heels: Is our God here, too?

We learn that whether we believe in you is not as important as what kind of God we believe you to be!

Help us to know you as more than a distant stranger who sits above us in the clouds, but rather as One who leads your children through lion dens, cross-cluttered hillsides, and rock-stoppered tombs. What is one more dark street to a God like that? Help us to know you as a God for even the darkest streets, homes, and lives; teach us to rely on you as a hand-in-hand companion, not a lucky charm that fails in the first hint of darkness.

Words of Light

God is . . . always ready to help in times of trouble. So we will not be afraid. (Psalm 46:1-2, GNB)

Random Violence

Ambushed

As random as lightning, evil ambushes. We are struck numb and grieving, certain we'll never feel safe again. O God, odds put us at equal risk of harm from stranger as from family. It doesn't matter. Can you believe it—they don't need to know us well enough to hate us?

Random, ambushing violation may not *be* personal, but it feels like it is. Calm quivering hearts; open drapes we close against the world. Tug at the heavy edges of our fear, and make us angry and active.

We are furious that we jump at every sound, cross streets at glimpses of strangers, and act like the darkness of hiding is preferable to light. And yet, O God of open windows and sunny hope, we are giving up on light if we concede defeat at the hands of snarling, weak punks and become hopeless, fearful. We may have been ambushed and could be again, but with your help we need not be fear's hostage.

We come not as students or scholars asking "why?" and "wherefore?" or investigating causes and cures for violence. We come just as your children, weighted down by fearful knowledge that evil waits to ambush us in our daily lives.

Despite that fear, we rely on your promise to set tables for us where, even in the presence of punks, you guard our feast and guide us through the valleys they prowl. An invitation to your picnic beside still waters, despite a cautious eye forward, is an invitation we want to accept.

Words of Light

The LORD is my shepherd . . . Though I walk through the valley . . . I will fear no evil. (Psalm 23:1,4, RSV)

In the Mood

Rude, crude, loud, mean. We live, O God, in an age of free-floating rage and hair-trigger tantrums. Daily news offers us litanies of violence, profound acts, like wars, and petty ones: an airline clerk is screamed at when flights are full; a commuter who takes the last seat is pummeled with upscale briefcases and expletives; someone who interprets Scripture differently is shot dead over a verse; movies, music, and elections play to our feeling of powerlessness. Rude, crude, loud, mean.

Like a breeze blowing across a landfill, this mean-spirited mood is stinking up our manners, homes, roads, churches, jokes, families, courts, entertainment, votes— wherever, O God, we are with our mistrust, divisiveness, arrogance, blame, justification.

Right, left, or center, we are whiny, intense, and rigid.

Heaven forbid we compromise. Tolerance? No way. *My* way, *my* say, or else. The zealous fringe, Lord, has moved center, and "Radical is Us" as we suspect and hiss at one another about everything. Quick to act and slow to negotiate, we overreact to problems, guaranteeing an equally fierce backlash. Mean, mean, mean.

Did it happen overnight, this shift from politeness to confrontation? Surely it's been coming on for a while. There are reasons: not enough jobs, money, or equality; traditions turned topsy-turvy; division, suspicion, and despair adopted as doctrines. Fear of change simply provided the trigger for aggression.

What, soul-knowing God, is the root of mean-spiritedness? Can it be personal, corporate, political, religious, and national selfishness? Could it be have-nots are breathing down the necks of haves shouting, "Share"?

Share? No way. Not wealth, power, position, or even room for another opinion. Mean, mean, mean.

Even if we don't want to do better, we need to, for we are harming ourselves by hating others in profound or petty ways! Peace is such a paradox, God of parables, that we often miss your point.

We'll pay closer attention now as you fill our bellies with hunger for compromise and even small bits of peace. Give us soft words to turn away wrath . . . before it leaves our mouths. Give us courage to peer into the darkness of our world and identify problems. Give us even greater courage to find hope in the darkness instead of more reasons to whine and spit at one another. Forgive us for using others as outlets for inner turmoil, the true source of this malaise.

And if we persist in this toxic mean-spiritedness, be ready to comfort us once we realize our emotional limp is from shooting ourselves in the foot. Mean, mean, mean.

Words of Light

You should all be like one big happy family, . . . loving one another with tender hearts and humble minds. . . . The Lord's face is hard against those who do evil. (1 Peter 3:8-12, TLB)

Gathering Up Your Lambs

With Rachel, Lord, we cry for the children. Shaken, punched, screamed at, molested, they are helpless rag dolls in the hands of adults.

Teach them to dodge flying fists, abusive words, and insistent fondlings. Teach them what it will take to cope in order to survive. Be their best childhood companion, for we have failed in that role, letting violence stalk and steal.

Comfort through foster parents who tuck them into safe beds; through play therapy where they learn that big dollies don't always lie to, trick, throw, burn, or rape little dollies in the playhouse of real life. Lullaby them with assurance that not all strangers, or kin, are bad.

Help them to learn to pass the abusing back to the abusers so as not to pass it on later to their own spouses and kids. *Hand it back, or pass it on, hand it back, or pass it on.* Lead all children, young and old, in this chant as if it were a jump rope rhyme; give them courage to hand it back.

Heal your "big kids," too, Lord, the adults crouched in memory closets as if they were still powerless children, although cloaked in grown-up skin. They wear a lifetime's misplaced shame. Coax them out with assurance that you will protect, that you will believe no matter how long it has taken for them to remember. Help us to support, protect, and believe.

We bow here, indicted by our silence, for it is partly our fault that we must bring broken children to you. We have not believed, intervened, protected, prosecuted. We have not made phone calls. We have not "interfered." Until too late, Lord. Too late, too late.

We promise to do better. In the meantime, we struggle to find praying words for the abusers. Stay with us until we can.

Words of Light

Whoever offends one of these little ones . . . better for him a millstone be hanged around his neck and that he were drowned in the sea. (Luke 17:2, NASB)

Thinking Backwards

Like a phonograph needle stuck in an antique groove, we can't get evil out of our minds. It is the root of so much misery, yet, O God, as difficult to spot as a tick on a dog. This won't be the last time we come to you with this troubling puzzle.

Work with us today, great Teacher, in a spelling lesson: We just discovered that *evil* is *live* spelled backwards.

How true. Others' evil intentions and actions do keep us from living as abundantly as you intend. And if we adopt evil as our guide, it actually destroys us.

What is *evil*? Is it the same as *sin*? Why are definitions of evil as varied as those who peddle it? How can we spot it? Do we dare call people evil? Aren't the ones who do evil just troubled, troublesome? How can anyone *live* with himself or herself after doing *evil*?

So many questions, O God, so much reluctance and revulsion at the definitions we avoid: fiend, vile, abomination, hellish, infamy, ungodliness, wanton, unclean, unutterable, unforgivable sin, atrocity, wicked, cursed. These hardly sound like small mistakes, simple errors in judgment we all make. Evil is something else, Lord, something else entirely.

Yet it sneaks up on us, drawing strength from our disbelief that it exists!

It is consistently sinful, subtle, and sly. It cloaks itself in charm, piety, kindness. We even feel silly talking with you now, Lord, half believing evil is something Hollywood created! Yet it is real, its effects all the evidence we need. Its practitioners assume the posture of willful ignorance and choose to disregard anyone or anything else. We are merely things in evildoers' paths to be used, misused, discarded as leftovers. Our pleas for mercy go as unheard as urgings that they repent or at least feel sorry. That, we wail into an abyss we don't want to see, is the difference: Evil knows no guilt and desires no growth. Unfeeling, uncaring, unmovable.

Hone our intuitions about how to spot evil. Inoculate us to its charm, O God, for despite its public-relations spin and seductive soft side, evil never lets its doers live. Evildoers self-destruct as they use others to prop up and preserve their own sick selves. Protect us from their intentions.

Words of Light

A worthless person, a wicked man, goes about with crooked speech, winks with his eyes, scrapes with his feet, points with his finger, with perverted heart devises evil, continually sowing discord; therefore, calamity will come upon him suddenly; in a moment he will be broken beyond healing. (Proverbs 6:12-15, RSV)

So are the ways of everyone who gains by violence; It takes away the life of its possessors. (Proverbs 1:19, NASB)

Enough

They are like Bambi pinned by car headlights; it's open season on women. Nothing new. Nothing new, God, except that now some descendants of Eve, the first woman to feel your creating touch, are saying, "Enough." They are taking back the night . . . and the day.

They seem like small things—random, casual harassment; porn; the assumption that "No" means "Maybe"; jokes. They seem like small things until taken as a whole that adds up to seeds of violence, ammunition in an unwinnable gender war.

Restrain those who take unfair sexual advantage of role and position. Capture and punish stalkers, touchers, molesters, rapists. The balance of power is never equal, and they have the edge in body strength and will to destroy. Chastise the ignorant, uninformed; their jokes and stereotypes demean everyone and mock your creation.

Bless and encourage your sons who treat women well. Fortify your daughters so they can become all you intended them to be without fear of harassment, assault. And if women are guilty of teasing and sending mixed signals, and men guilty of insensitivity and gender terrorism, restore our belief that under your teaching hand, tomorrow can be a better, nonviolent day. We can learn; we can be better to one another.

Male and female, you created us, O God, and you said it was good. May it be so again.

Words of Light

I am helpless, overwhelmed, in deep distress; . . . Deliver my life from their power! (Psalm 25:16-21, TLB)

Poster Truth

"*If,*" a poster asks, "*women in pretty clothes are asking to be raped, are men in classy business suits asking to be robbed?*"

A modern riddle, God of tough questions. "Of course not," we laugh at first. Absurd. Yet we live as if it were true that women set themselves up for violation. Sagely we observe after reading of rape or attempted rape, "She should've known that wearing a skirt (sweater, bathing suit, T-shirt) would get her in trouble."

Yet, O God, we cry in protest, what about old women in lace-up brogues, corsets, and trifocals? ill, retarded, helpless ladies in nursing homes? defenseless little girls? What about them? Rape is not about your gift of sex. It's not even about lust. Rape is an act of violence.

Remind your daughters that they have rights: to say no, to not blame themselves, to assume *someone* will believe them. Jostle your sons so they understand that "no" means "no"; that stereotypes of women on billboards, commercials, and movie and television screens are lies; and that mixed messages can be dealt with in better ways than assault.

Send women into the world savvy and vigilant. Teach them how to spot predators who use sex as a weapon of domination and destruction. Make their feet fleet, their fists mighty. When that doesn't protect, keep your daughters alive to tell the tale in voices that demand protection, justice.

Words of Light

Deliver me, O LORD, from evil men. (Psalm 140:1, RSV)

Role Models? Not!

From political assembly to pulpit, a frenzied call to hatred in the name of God and country rings from sea to shining sea. Our great melting pot is singed on the bottom as we wave flags and lift prayers for freedom, but, forgive us, as we also make darn sure it's best for me and mine. The call goes out: Lift a prayer to smear others; raise a flag to bludgeon.

Oh, dear God, we are bashing and bullying for you.

Worry plus *world problems* minus *our own good sense* multiplied by *skillful recruiters* equals a mob intent, if not on converting others, then on annihilating them politically, religiously, financially. Even literally. Men, women, and children spread makeup and gilt over their intentions to overpower and destroy. Slogans and verses set a cadence for our night marches against brother and sister whom we've randomly labeled "enemy."

We blow up these enemies first with words, then with firebombs.

Where are you, God of peace, in the call to shun, destroy those who are "different"? What about "created equal"? What about lions and lambs together?

Yet we are terrified to speak up or even don a bumper sticker suggesting *"Hate is not a family value."* (We remember what happened to your son when he spoke up.) Peace is as dangerous as righteous, patriotic mobs. Forgive our cowardice then and now. Help us to turn deaf ears to calls to hate, no matter how carefully camouflaged in red-white-and-blue bunting or how piously delivered with head-bowed postures. Can a ravenous false prophet in sheep's clothing be a leader of yours? We are wrestling with that claim.

Words of Light

For there are many . . . empty talkers and deceivers . . . who must be silenced because they are upsetting whole families, teaching things they should not teach, for the sake of sordid gain. (Titus 1:10-13, NASB)

Lightning Rods

Kids kill and are killed in record numbers, shepherd God. Like lambs going to slaughter through violent lives, they roam, no matter how swank and upscale the addresses.

We fear them but must help them, the violent little kids and murderous, remorseless teens. We confess, ashamed and wary of facing the truth, that we have allowed it to happen. We polluted our own backyard by ignoring families and kids in need. They had no time for childhood while learning to forage for food and shelter and to dodge bullets on playgrounds and porches.

Kids who've been neglected and abused and who now abuse one another and us are lightning rods for violent society. These kids get our attention as the root causes of their violence never have. When faced with evil, the kids misinterpreted it, assuming it was in them. We preferred not to know how bad their lives were, settling for prejudices and assumptions about race, finance, culture. How in error we have been, how unfair and hurtful, how simplistic to relegate meanness to *others'* backyards. Collective, if not personal guilt indicts us here, God of justice.

In the spirit of apology, we are ready to listen, to help kids. Teach us ways to reach past our fear. Give us creative ideas and strength to carry them out. Too many of our efforts are superficial, like pouring fertilizer on rocks around plants, not touching roots at all. We want to do more than provide cosmetic touches, more than paint over the graffiti.

Help us to read *between* the lines of graffiti and gang markings to see the tales of loneliness, the need to belong, and the justified rage at inequity. We can teach alternatives to blowing someone away, torching a car, shooting a stranger. We want streets and families to be safe for all, even for the kids we fear with their wild hair, loud music, guns in backpacks. We can help.

But, Lord, we protest, troubled kids are hard to love, hard to get close to. We confess to major reluctance, disgust. Let this be a first clue about where we need to get involved. Help us to reach past barriers of appearance and bluff—even bullets—to young hearts and minds that can change. Inspire us with stories of those who take your message through caring action to streets, schools, and playgrounds, to kids who yearn for someone strong in ways other than fists or guns. Can it be us? Go with us as we try.

Words of Light

Children are a gift of the LORD. (Psalm 127:3, NASB)

If they are sad, share their sorrow. (Romans 12:15, TLB)

Masks

Evil has gotten itself spiffed up, hiding behind masks of charm, success, piety. We're getting better at ferreting out evil, God of truth. Seems like every week another "good" one falls, another mask is lifted. "High time," we say, even as we mourn the unmasking of those we'd thought we could trust, admire. *Reveal their deceptions; comfort our betrayed hearts.*

Every day is Halloween in many lives, but masks of niceness cover monsters. We expect nice people sometimes to wear monster masks; we find, though, that "good"-person masks conceal bully monsters who satisfy their needs at others' expense. *Expose their secrets in your searing light of truth; heal our shocked minds.*

Often, sadly, monsters' families are good at keeping secrets even from themselves, for when you live with a monster, it's either lie or suffer in the telling. O God of deliverance, be the first to believe those who dare speak about clever impersonators, and unstop our ears for truths we don't want to hear. *Forgive our disbelief.*

O God of kept promises, forgive those who, preferring mask to reality, punish tattlers who believe that "truth . . . will set you free." Give us courage to tattle, to tell. Keep us from cynicism and mistrust, the fertile ground where evil thrives. Remind us that plants grow best once noxious weeds are laid bare to wither in the sun. So, too, are we most likely to flourish when evil deceit is exposed. *Keep us hopeful seekers of truth.*

Words of Light

"You are like whitewashed tombs, which on the outside appear beautiful, but inside are full of dead men's bones and all uncleanness. . . . You too outwardly appear righteous, . . . but inwardly you are full of hypocrisy and lawlessness." (Matthew 23:27-28, NASB)

Take no part in the unfruitful works of darkness, but instead expose them. . . . For it is a shame even to speak of the things that they do in secret; . . . but when anything is exposed by the light, it becomes visible. . . . (Ephesians 5:11-13, RSV)

Horse Thieves:
A Personal Note

Horse thieves used to be hanged, O God, a practice of which I approve: We were just robbed while coming home from vacation. Clothes, souvenirs, computer, briefcase, notes, and new manuscripts, gone. Shards from a broken car window are all I have to take home. And a sense of violation.

Although I have the law on my side, I am in danger again, this time from my own hand, from my desire for retaliation. I would repay violence with violence if I could get my hands on the thugs who took our belongings.

My eagerness to do violence is frightening, catching me as off guard as the robbery itself. I, too, am capable of inflicting pain if given a chance, and, I confess, I want a chance as I look now with suspicion at my world.

Caution us against fearing and penalizing all whose age, hair, clothes, race, and beliefs differ from ours, as if they are automatically the enemy, thieves in the night. We would nail to the wall anyone who seems the least bit suspicious. We would make ourselves, Lord, judge, jury, and executioners.

After that first appropriate surge of fury in the wake of violence, calm us. Send us to lead volunteers rather than vigilantes. Send us to read in schools, to lead literacy classes, to tend clinics, to mend playgrounds, to befriend children.

Help us to find the courage to bind up rather than tear down. Otherwise, we will become what we abhor: thieves of rights.

Help us to prevent robberies—all crime—with early intervention, rather than waiting to pick up stolen pieces too late. We have never needed you more, Lord, than in these burglar-alarmed times, when we long to toss a hanging rope over a tree limb and call it even. Teach us your new way.

Words of Light

Be angry but do not sin. (Ephesians 4:26, RSV)

Side by Side

Someone I care about very much is a victim of violence, making me one, too. A senseless, violent act shattered beliefs, faith, and security, Lord, not to mention our relationship. How can I help? I want to be a channel of your healing, empowering love.

Hear my prayers on behalf of those, loved ones and strangers, who cannot, now, trust your benevolence. Guide them back to you through us.

Help me to know what to do and say. And show me when my best gift may simply be companionable silence.

Help me not to turn away from physical touch, a hug, an embrace, for I know I sometimes do that. And help me not to take it personally when someone turns away from my touch, for that happens, too.

Help me to keep quiet about my own griefs when bitterness and cynicism rule conversation, when fear replaces pleasure, and lust for vengeance colors days, sunrise to sunset. For these moments, this pain, are not mine. Give me patience to wait my turn to grieve.

Help me to find a spot close enough to be supporting but not intruding; close enough to listen but not so close as to stifle grieving, shock-laden rage and emotional outbursts, for they are healing. Let the words flow over my head, in one ear and out the other, for I know this is necessary transition, a temporary place. Let me be a sounding board, a patient audience for volumes of outrage and pain.

Hear my prayer on behalf of those who cannot, now, trust your benevolence. Let me be a channel of your mind-changing comfort. Above all, Lord, help me to find words and gestures to assure those in pain that I believe, for I do.

Words of Light

Two are better off than one. . . . If one of them falls down, the other can help him up. . . . If it is cold, two can sleep together and stay warm. (Ecclesiastes 4:9-11, GNB)

From the Rubble, Hope: Remembering Oklahoma City

It took a bomb in the gut to bring us to our knees before you, O God. The kaleidoscope of life turned too fast and our world was suddenly not what we thought it was. Spring colors became faded and dull when we saw them through the lens of grief during prime-time television.

We who stand at a distance from personal loss, as the dust settles in Oklahoma, are mourning a death—the death of innocence. Evil is alive and well and stands proudly over the remains of our naivete. How vain to think we were different from countries where bombs burst in air at the whim of disagreement; how self-absorbed we are to ignore the symptoms of hate let loose among us; how terrifying it is to see with wide-open eyes the world we've created.

Forgive not our innocence but our indifference. Forgive our silence that let a fringe move to the middle—of our country, our minds, and, yes, we confess, our souls. Hate has become a national pastime.

You were the first to gasp at this astonishing outbreak of hate. You were the first to weep at the senseless loss of life it spawned. O God, who redeemed even a crucifixion into resurrection, can you make from this random tragedy something useful, something upon which we can build?

Guide us as we search through the rubble of mind and spirit where innocence is buried, and help us to find hope— hope that a wake-up call is all we need in order to turn from the darkness of hate and the fear that feeds it, to a light where babies aren't bombed and bombers aren't cheered.

Words of Light

Let us then pursue what makes for peace and for mutual up-building. (Romans 14:19, RSV)

Diagnosis

Weary, yet sleepless. Justified, yet uneasy. Vigilant, yet fearful. Protected, yet threatened. The list of conflicting symptoms is endless as our bodies warn us of dis-ease, O great Physician. We fear that if left untreated, this malady of contagious violence that saps our energy and races our hearts will lead to our demise. Yet, we confess, we put off taking care of it, because it has become so alluring and intoxicating.

Help us to recognize finger pointing, name-calling, fist raising, person bashing, and fear peddling as warning signs of malignancy that settles in our very marrow if we let it. My God, no wonder our bodies are consumed with dis-ease: We've caught the random, vitriolic hate going around. *Have mercy on us, for we gave it to ourselves.*

Touch us with a healing hand of restraint. Soothe us with glimpses of peace. Dose us with empathy, vision, and energy for ways to settle disputes other than hate-spreading, knee-jerk, hair-trigger violence, from the profound to the petty. And when we whine our complaints, come to us in our feverish crusades and furies, and ask us, as Jesus asked the man at the pool of Bethesda, *"Do you want to be healed?"*

Maybe yes, maybe no, we confess, Lord of swirling waters. The first step in healing is being awakened to reality, the reality that all is not well with our souls. Weep with us if we prefer to get in a last word, a final blow. It is within our power to find a cure for this malady. All we have to do is decide whether we want to be healed or to live with the symptoms of dis-ease.

Words of Light

[Jesus] said to him, "Do you want to be healed?" (John 5:6, RSV)

If sinners entice you, do not consent, . . . for their feet run to evil, and . . . they set an ambush for their own lives. (Proverbs 1:10-18, RSV)

Overtime Fear

We work in vulnerable spots on the job, God of toil and tasks, ready to take cover as we scan to see who might erupt in random workplace violence. It can be small violence with hollering voices and flying fists, or big violence with guns, deadly intentions, and grievances over bullet-spattered bodies. Homicide is the second leading cause of death on the job, Lord. Small or big, violence occurs in presidential suites and on factory floors, touching millions of us, numbers not in corporate reports.

There is much to feel violent about when jobs change rapidly and overseers demand that we keep up with that change. Impersonal and disloyal management, boring jobs, wage freezes, layoffs, and threatened downsizing infuriate us.

We retaliate first by slacking off, next by not showing up and bilking the system, and finally by violence. O God, we have had it.

It is scary to witness workplace violence, big or little. It is scary, we confess, when we discover within us violent urges to flail and lash out at anyone in our paths. Could we shoot a boss who fired us? Could we damage property in revenge for layoffs? Could we destroy reputations of those who cheat or lie about us? Sure, Lord, sure.

Show us instead how to cool off, talk it out. Help us to name our frustrations in creative ways. Teach us to channel anger so we won't hurt others or ourselves, physically or professionally, with violent outbursts.

Teach management to provide for conflict resolution rather than to sweep aside frustrations like paper scraps and production-line castoffs. Remind them that untended tempers can affect the almighty bottom line, costing billions of dollars from unchecked violence, another figure unfit to report.

Words of Light

Jesus said, "No more of this!" (Luke 22:51, RSV)

Shifting Sands

The day, O God, we went to war in the desert, I bought three cartons of ice cream. Lemon, mocha, and fudge brownie. During the news, I ate the frozen comfort. It wasn't until I heard the click of my spoon against the bowl that I paid attention to the cadence of my eating: hut, two, three, four, eating as if going to war.

Lord, we love war, ultimate random violence against strangers we don't have to care about—strategies, mockups, projections, tallies, and replays. We love the *zing* of contest, doing our best against the odds, doing our best to strike first, fastest, and proudest. *Help us to know what issues justify our military, battleground, and warring expertise.* In the deadly game of "who threw the first stone," country to country, you are the only lineman who can make that call.

We love war, but we keep that a secret even from ourselves, so we won't notice our own strident calls to arms beneath our prayers for peace. We love war so much we will battle with friend, family, and neighbor over whether our country should wage one, even arguing about wars long past! We make our relationships miniwars. Isn't there a better way?

We love war but spurn its cost, squirming in discomfort at flag-covered coffins lumbering across our television screens. I dread for both of us what we may see in modern wars, Creator Lord: images of your daughters as sacrifice of war. (Do we have equal rights to die?)

Guard us from the despair that dictates fighting is the only way to resolve differences, contain villains, and bring peace. Remind us that patriotism is also about cleaning up our decayed cities; patching up our broken families; mending our tumbledown morals and morales; and reclaiming our neighborhoods from our homegrown tyrants: poverty, hunger, and violence.

Lead us in parades about equality and justice for all and
a voice for everyone, not about military victory alone.
Cheer us on to cross the finish line of the enterprise we began short centuries ago: creating a melting pot of diverse
people, O God; a glorious stew of savory ideas and notions;
not a bland, one-flavor pudding with one thought indivis-
ible for all. Bless our diversity and differences, and help us
to become comfortable with them.

Judge us on the quality of our protest against injustice
and evil, as well as against simplistic solutions on both
sides of debate. Help us to learn to reject war—personal
ones, global ones, little ones, big ones. We must avoid the
final one. And if we must fight bullet-and-bomb wars for
liberty, for protection, for release of the captive, please,
Lord of doves and olive branches, rid us of our love for
those wars.

Words of Light

Preserve me from [the] violent . . . who . . . stir up wars continually. (Psalm 140:1-2, RSV)

Kicking Mother Nature's Shins

Sharing is not a natural state, Creator God, as you know. We don't share toys when we are kids, and we don't share land, sea, and air with "lesser" creatures when we are adults. We reinterpret your advice to "subdue" creation rather than fulfill your plan for us to be its caretakers.

We walk roughshod over fellow creatures' homes and habitats and hunt what we do not need, lying to ourselves that it doesn't matter, that it isn't connected to other violence around us. No wonder we do the same to one another. We have little respect for life, little reverence for others' rights and places in it. It's the same attitude: *I need only think about me.* Forgive us.

Teach us reverence for all creation. Slow our devouring appetites. Caution us against using up future generations' resources, especially since *we* will not feel the deprivation. Remind us that a selfish heart is its own deprivation. Hold us accountable for raping land and fouling water in the name of progress. Lead us past vacant buildings and ghost towns that mock our drive for more, more, new, new. Teach us the wisdom in reusing, converting, reclaiming.

Teach us to love restraint. Show us the pleasure in making a ball of string, a wad of foil, a heap of compost; in letting fireflies go; in preserving and protecting. Make us savers, not wasters, creators of a chronic random violence that falls like acid rain on our own heads! Reconnect us to the roots and tides from which we came and to which we will go again. Remind us just how earthy we are!

We might wind up king of the mountain only to discover that the mountain we have built with our violence is a slag heap of stagnant leftovers.

Words of Light

Thou didst set the earth on its foundations, . . . The earth is satisfied with the fruit of thy work. . . . O LORD, how manifold are thy works! In wisdom has thou made them all; the earth is full of thy creatures. (Psalm 104:5,13,24 RSV)

Bomb Shelters

"Bombs bursting in air" is not just a colorful line from a song, O God. It is a time-lapse moment in our daily lives as we watch the innocent die on prime time. War-zone refugees and soldiers, subway commuters and airline passengers, school-bus kids and holiday vacationers, and now our neighbors in the heartland have become fodder to feed crazed minds that randomly toss death in our faces for the sake of a cause, a grudge, a point.

A fire fighter carrying a bomb-blasted baby has become a poster for our times, and we are frightened. We buried trust with that baby and now look askance at stranger *and* neighbor. We hesitate before traveling, yet fear the casual, random blast of violence if we stay home. We are afraid for our country and ashamed that we ignored warning signs of rot in our own backyard, sea to shining sea. Aftershocks reverberate still.

What to do now, O God? Retreat or regroup?

Not so many years ago, we dug bomb shelters. Like moles, we burrowed beneath fear, stockpiling rations and plans for a better tomorrow. Shall we go back down or stay topside as targets?

Help us to find security *above ground* by becoming peacemakers. Fortify us for standing up to hatemongers. Give us David-strength and more than a handful of stones of creative ideas. Guide us as we ponder "all things work together for good," for where is "good" in the bomb rubble of terrorism, home or abroad? *Awareness, a wake-up call to make peace* is as close as we can come, a foundation sturdy enough that no bomb can destroy.

Words of Light

We know that in everything God works for good. (Romans 8:28, RSV)

Unsightly Growth: A Personal Note

Like a wrung-out dishrag, dear God, I worry that your love is twisted in the hands of some of your followers. Picketers on all sides claim you as coach. Finger-pointers do it in your name. Are you cheering or crying at the acts of violence credited to you?

It's easy to understand, if not approve of, adults taking up arms over issues. Hate is heady elixir. Children, though, are a shock. Last week, dear God, their hate hit me at a picket line I had to cross. Are we right or wrong to ignore chanting mobs? We worry about them but don't get involved until personally touched, as I was by a lump in my breast. Its possibilities were ice in the mind.

Were you the one who strung a human chain between me and the clinic? Were you cheering as they spat at me in your name? You were, *if* I am to believe the songs, chants, prayers, and crosses brandished at me. You were there *if* I am to believe the curses hurled at me for entering a clinic mistakenly targeted for abortion protest. You were there *if* I am to believe the times I heard your name damning me. May it not be true, I plead.

"Dear God," I prayed then and now, "keep me from hating as much as I am hated. Help us to negotiate, resolve divisive issues. But is *this* your way?"

Prayer in my heart, fire in my eye, I managed to get into the building past a chanting, catsup-blood-smeared child. She was waiting when I came out, my spirits soaring with good news, thanks on my lips.

"You," the child hollered, brandishing a Bible in my face and interrupting my grateful prayer, "are going to hell." No, I shook my head, not going: I was already there, my lump the only benign growth on the corner.

Words of Light

Anyone who says he is a Christian but doesn't control his sharp tongue is just fooling himself, and his religion isn't worth much. (James 1:26, TLB)

Let love be without hypocrisy. (Romans 12:9, NASB)

A Big Kids' Riddle

The *b* in today's alphabet soup stands neither for Big Bouncing Ball nor for Barney, the kind-hearted purple dinosaur who's loved his way into the hearts of small children. No, Lord who invited children to come close, *b* stands for Barney Bashing.

Hate crimes have hit the playground in a metaphor of our times.

"I hate you, you hate me, we're worst friends like friends should be. With a great big punch and a kick from me to you, won't you say you hate me too?" With the same tune as the "love you" version, it takes its place in hate-full events where we adults target this sappy, purple love-freak—morning talk show, late night comedy routine, office water cooler conversation, prime-time analysis, and finger-pointing sermon!

For unexplainable reasons, O God, love is suspect, cooperation and tolerance are heresy, and positive solutions are annoying! Even as we wail about declining moral fiber, we are the first to shoot an arrow of spite at peace promoters, even ones dressed in fuzzy purple. Why are we so threatened? There is more to this, I fear, than boredom with preschoolers' best friend: We love to be mean! Lord, Lord, do we dare become like little children as you require? No one's safe, even in childhood.

We're a mixed-up people, surely not the people you envisioned at the moment of creation. We distort and torque love, gentleness, hope, peace. We crucify those who promote them. We dare not stand too near this purple dinosaur for, like your Son, he's a lightning rod for mean-spirited vibes from stand-up late show pundits or prime time news commentators! We ignore your efforts to teach us to follow the simple way of kids that you seem to favor. We even turn on a purple toy!

Like little kids, we have even more questions: *Why* do some "big kids" hate so much? *Why* is their hate accepted, delighted in? *Why* are gentle folk picked on, persecuted, resented? Your Son found out firsthand, and we bow in shame for not having learned from that.

Where, God of future hope, are we to be in this boiling-over of hate-as-fun? Heaven forbid singing "I Hate You" loudest, or ridiculing and begrudging what is hopeful, even in singsong ditties and simple skits of sharing and sweetness. You do, indeed, work in mysterious ways. What, then, shall we do about those kicking you in the shins?

Words of Light

I will praise you, my God. . . . Let each generation tell its children what glorious things he does. (Psalm 145:1,4, TLB)

Violence:
Up Close and Personal

Conversation

From the beginning of creation, O God, we have hidden. Shame hid us behind fig leaves; guilt, behind rocks and lies; fear, behind bluster. Now we are hiding behind secrets of what someone did to us.

Whether we are adults who are newly violated or children who put away terrible truth long, long ago, secrecy makes puppets of us, holding us back from abundant life. But, O God, dare we come clean, slink out of hiding, and tattletale the truth? Will you protect us if we break silence?

We hear your assurance. We hear you calling us yet again as you did in the garden, when we are renaming dreams, on sun-blinded dusty roads, and adrift on wave-tossed seas. We are grateful that you are always seeking us, Lord of the lost, and we stand up to shout, "Here, here! We are here!"

Lean close, for we can hardly bear to whisper even to you how we've been made to keep silent, Lord—the threats, the pain, the lies. And if anyone knew what really happened, we fear they'd turn away. Be the first to hear it. Reassure us that you won't flinch from what we say . . .

There, that feels better. We feel lighter, clearer-headed. We feel you draw us close and point beyond secrets to truth that sets us free: Darkness *never* puts out light. In that truth we can now talk to others who will help us in practical ways. They will be the hands and feet of a God who wants us out of hiding and free.

Words of Light

When anything is exposed by the light it becomes visible. (Ephesians 5:13, RSV)

Soap and Water

No water is hot enough, no blankets thick enough, to cleanse and warm me. I was ambushed. "Rape" has been written forever across my soul like lines on a police report.

I call for help by day; I cry out in the night before thee. (Psalm 88:1, RSV)

Where were you, God of hollow promises, when I was running for my life? Where were you when I clawed and fought under threat of death? Where were you in the soiling of my soul and the rending of my body? Where were you in the chill aftermath when evil triumphed by escaping? Why did you abandon me?

My soul is full of troubles, and my life draws near to Sheol. (v. 3, RSV)

Can we mend this rending of my body and my soul? Trust and faith, God of other times, were raped, too. They lie tangled among leftovers like torn clothes of a life forever changed. Why didn't you prevent it? I thought your angels watched over me. I didn't see a single one.

I am counted with those who go down to the pit. I am a [woman] who has no strength. (v. 4, NKJV)

Send me partners and friends to prop me up. Send advocates to work the system, so that justice will be served. Send me vigilantes who will ensure justice if the system stalls, victimizing me again. In time, O God, I may mellow and forgive. Right now, I would lead the vigilante attack. Accept my rage. Help me to know that fire of anger is as cleansing as a hot bath.

Rouse yourself. . . . Why are you looking the other way? (v. 14, LB)

Dilute my anger at you with our mingled tears. There were moments when I heard you weeping with me, felt your hands as fists around mine. There are moments when, as through a camera shutter, I glimpse you as my companion.

Rise up, . . . come and help us . . . by your constant love. (Psalm 44:26, TLB)

Give me the courage to face and name my injuries so that they'll not fester and become permanent disabilities. Stand with me when I accuse and seek justice. Bolster me against others' desires that I not tell in order to protect a name, a reputation, privacy.

Who will stand up for me against evildoers, . . . those who do wickedness? He has brought back their wickedness upon them, And will destroy them in their evil. . . . (Psalm 94:16,23, NASB)

God of foot washings and river bathings, cleanse me of the dirt left from someone's hate. Remind me that it doesn't belong to me, no matter how personal it feels. Fortify the boundaries of the place where the assault occurred, so I'll not be afraid to go there again. Send your spirit to blow through and clean the spaces, like spring winds blow away winter dust. Each time I feel your breezes, I can say, "With this wind, I accept your cleansing." In that moment, I will know I am reunited with you despite the vileness that attempted to separate us.

I called on thy name . . . Out of the lowest pit. Thou hast heard my voice, . . .Thou didst draw near when I called on thee; . . . Thou hast redeemed my life. (Lamentations 3:55-58, NASB)

Words of Light

(Psalms 88 and 94; Psalm 44:15-26; Lamentations 3:55-58; 2 Samuel 13:1-22)

Liar, Liar, Mind's on Fire

I found the verse, "wives, submit," but it was difficult to read through tears. Secret tears, God of truth, for I dare not show pain even to myself. To stay in this union is to avoid truth.

So I explain to those who wonder about bruises: "I fell down the stairs, ran into a door." I explain isolation: "I really don't want to go . . . no time." I explain staying: "I believe in marriage 'til death do us part." Is our inertia as dangerous as the violence we lie about to cover up, especially to kids?

We lie so convincingly to ourselves that we outstay not only our welcome but sometimes our very lives. We wonder: When does commitment become trap? Do we cause the violence to us? Do *you* think we deserve steely rejection; stinging slaps; perverse, shameful couplings? Do *you* think we deserve to be spied on, stalked, belittled, ridiculed?

We wish you would rescue us, for we feel abandoned, even as we suspect it is our inertia that keeps us captive. We are grateful for times when we feel your rescuing insistence that we get out. Show us words different from "submit" in your Word, words like "choose life," while we're deciding what to do.

Help us to make peace with the choices that brought us here. Help us to become wise, skilled, intuitive, self-valuing, and strong, so that we do not repeat those choices. Remind us of shelters, escape routes; give us insight to know we need one. Be our guide, God of pilgrim people, on a path to new life. We accept the truth—*that* is what we deserve, not violence in the name of love.

Words of Light

I have set before you life and death, blessing and curse; therefore, choose life, that you and your descendants may live. . . . (Deuteronomy 30:19, RSV)

Exit Lines:
Courage for the Journey

This is not a safe place. I don't know how I know, O God; I just do. There is, though, such a difference between knowing and going. I feel paralyzed with trying to make sense out of unbelievable pain. *Help those at the mercy of pure meanness to understand that action often needs to precede knowledge.* We are further imperiled by indecision; help us to know *when* to go and to believe that *where* will become possible. *"Why?"* comes later.

Then, God of daring escapes, make us skillful and crafty in flights for survival. Assure us that we will find sanctuary first in your keeping and then in the hands of others who intercede, protect. During the flight, we will aim at your voice calling us forward. Bolster us with the grip of your hand pulling ours when we falter in old habits, fear, or guilt.

And when we look over our shoulders and see pursuers, stiffen our resolve and send us support: We will not return to lives of intimidation, hiding, lying. Steady us in our grief, for we have to leave some good things behind, too. In time, we can sort that out. For now, we'll just keep moving, keep moving, keep moving.

We are grateful for your presence during bleak days of indecision; too long we denied the need for flight. Protect others like us not only from violence surrounding them but from their need not to know. In some dark moment, bring us into their minds. We are grateful, God of history, that you are always calling us—in the garden, from trees, from boats—and now from this place—this marriage, this family—to come, to be more. It is as scary as it is hopeful to hear it.

Accept our exit line, "I'm coming," as the prayer of gratitude it is.

Words of Light

Shake off the dust from your feet as you leave. (Matthew 10:14, RSV)

He gives strength to the weary and increases the power of the weak. (Isaiah 40:29, NIV)

Watch Out!
Wreck around the Bend

Sometimes, Guardian of our lives, we barely make it to safety. We made it this time, though, and a violent, degrading union is receding in the past like a ten-car pile-up in the rearview mirror. *Help me to forgive myself for staying so long.*

We believed we were as powerless and of as little value as we were treated and told we were. We believed we deserved violence in subtle and not-so-subtle ways, from ideas to words to fists to weapons. We believed you would punish us if we broke vows and commitment. *Thank you for your other words: You are mine.*

We heard you calling over the persuasive violence of our lives and knew you intended us to be victors, not victims. *Thank you for your question, "Do you want to be healed?" Thank you for your promise, "Take up your mat and walk."* We do and we did. We've made it this far, God of swirling, restoring waters, and we are grateful for another chance. Thank you for inspiring, fortifying, and nudging us this far.

It's when ultimate disaster almost strikes but finally doesn't that we shudder and shake, like when we drive around a sharp curve just as cars ahead pile up in the fog. A minute earlier, we'd have been dead center. Curves and fog can hide stalled traffic from view, just as fear and conditioning can keep us from seeing calamity in relationships that would destroy us, children you created in your image. *We are grateful for second, third chances to be that child of yours. Help us to know we are worthy. Make us wiser from here on out.*

Words of Light

Forgetting what lies behind, . . . I press on. (Philippians 3:13-14, RSV)

[Jesus] said to him, "Do you want to be healed? . . . Pick up your pallet, and walk." (John 5:6,8, RSV)

Can You Believe It?

Do we need to recite to you the long list of the crimes your littlest ones endure? Do we need to mention, God who beckoned them to your knee, the threats made to ensure silence? the pets hurt or killed as reminders? the blind eyes, deaf ears, silent mouths of those who suspect but don't tell? Do we need to carry to you all the little broken bodies with flat, wary eyes that need your healing care, your gentle hand laid upon them? How it must break your heart to see them flinch from even your touch. But some touch robs, taking away childhood, so forgive their rejection of yours. *Help us to be healers of this broken trust on your behalf.*

In these enlightened times when the taboos against mentioning abuse are falling as quickly as bowling pins under the rapidly moving spirit of concern, kindle our indignation on the little ones' behalf. Educate us so we can't hide behind "I can't believe it" when children come forward to connect well-known names to unspeakable crimes. *Give us courage to couple belief with a resounding call for accountability and justice. Make us advocates.*

But right now, God of miraculous escapes, of Red Seas and bulrushes, what about the little ones enduring childhood at the hands of those hiding not only in alleys and slums but also behind designer homes, public office, Bible study, wit, and winning manner? Can you break down the doors to terror and save them? We are praying that they can hold on until help arrives. Go now, Lord. Hurry; we are on your heels.

Words of Light

"Whoever receives one child like this in my name is receiving me; and whoever receives me is not receiving me, but him who sent me." (Mark 9:37, NASB)

Asking for It? Not!

"Shut up and eat," he hissed, tossing kiddy meals at a trio of little kids. Their hands were not quick enough, Lord of little ones, so fries tumbled to the floor and burgers undid themselves across suddenly frozen laps. On the backswing, he caught their faces, "Okay, you asked for it." Three slaps faster than you could say "pass the salt."

There are few absolutes, Author of most of them, but surely one is that it is never, never okay to hurt a child. In the name of discipline, in the name of love, in the name of teaching lessons, in the name of easing some kind of adult angst from leftover pain. No kid ever asks for hitting, beating, slapping, ridiculing, groping, or molesting. With Rachel, we wail for those who get it.

Down on our knees, Lord, we are begging on their behalf for your intervention and guidance for how we can help. Put your restraining hand on hands that lash out and "give you what you asked for." If they persist in dishing it out, give us courage to act, for *they* are asking for it: restraint, prosecution, prevention, and punishment to fit their crimes. As your hands and feet, we will intervene, report, jot down license numbers, make anonymous tips, whatever it takes to save the kids.

When we hesitate to get involved, make us hear what your little ones, O God, are really asking for: our help.

Words of Light

"Which of you, if his son asks for . . . a fish, will give him a snake? . . . How much more will your Father in heaven give good gifts to those who ask him!" (Matthew 7:9-11, NIV)

"I have come that they may have life, and that they may have it more abundantly." (John 10:10, NKJV)

Easy Prey

*(In memory of Michael and Alex Smith,
and all the others)*

Your name, O God, is being called out in horror above sirens edging through a nation's heart. *O God, O God, no.*

Two little boys became poster children for family violence, finally drawing our attention to generations of unresolved abuse that eventually can claim small lives coast to coast, uptown and down. *Forgive our apathy.* Help us to see signs of trouble lying in wait. Make us reach out.

We wish our myths about bogeyman were always true, and we mourn the fact that danger mostly wears a family face, generation to generation. *O God, protect us from our own.*

And what of mercy? We cannot bear hearing those who harm their kids beg for mercy. How dare they? How could you consider granting it? Should we? *Soften our hearts but not our minds and laws. Help us to keep it straight: Mercy is not exemption. Have mercy upon their souls.*

What are we to believe about you when darkness seems, if not victorious, at least triumphant? Give us a sign that evil will not have the last word over these small bodies. God forbid that evil can live on in our bitterness. *Instead, give us patience to let grief do its healing wonder so we'll not stay stuck here.* Move us on to lightning-bug summers and snowball-and-sledding winters, where first we will kneel and then rise to dance in tribute to the children whose violations and deaths diminish us all.

And as we do, God of mercy, stay near. It is hard to offer even a leftover prayer for the twisted ones who break our hearts by hurting children. Forgive our miserly compassion.

Words of Light

The face of the Lord is against those who do evil. (1 Peter 3:12, NIV)

God, being rich in mercy, made us alive. (Ephesians 2:4-5, NASB)

Bleached Rainbows

(By a child raped by her father, who broke a kitten's neck to ensure silence)

Dear God,
　What I fear
　is not
　the freight train
　hurling . . . crashing . . . shattering
　pain of grief
　that sends the voice upward
　to displace clouds.
　No . . .
　. . . what I fear is the quietness
　of an ordinary morning
　a diffusion
　of sunlight gently warming
　unnamed tears
　shed before
　shed before and still
　by all the others
　who have watched from their windows
　all the ordinary mornings
　that punctuate our living
　with commas
　not
　exclamation points.
　What I fear
　is not the sharpness
　of an outcry
　or being swept away
　by roaring thundering waves
　but the softness
　of the early morning sky

and I seek a pain
to distract me
from ordinary
mournings.

Dear God, whom we cannot call "father," comfort your
children with touch that heals, not harms. Enfold them in
a loving embrace that frees, not binds. Their world turned
bad in a split second of dark deeds that bleached color
even from rainbows and made sunrises into mournings.

Our prayers come in dusty cartoon puffs of grief and
rage. Our dry bones rattle as we shake a trembling fist at
you, God who promised to lift us up on eagles' wings and
guide us through valleys. Now hope, like innocence, lies
buried with trust, no better than fool's gold at the end of fa-
ble rainbows.

Words of Light

He who troubles his own house will inherit wind. (Proverbs
11:29, NASB)

Tattletales

Like spidery etchings on plaster walls, cracks in tiny toddler bones spread top to bottom of the X-ray film, skull to shin. Yet another little one at risk right before our eyes. (We'd suspected what science confirmed.) Reports can be filed, intervention and help offered. Change is possible now that truth is told. *Be with doctors, great Physician, who read danger "between the lines" of perfectly kept baby books by allegedly adoring parents. Give doctors courage to stick to their guns; insist that we support them.*

We say "allegedly" adoring parents, for appearances are deceiving when adoration turns to anger—pummeling, flailing anger—when no one is looking. The family claims "accident," shaking their heads and smiling indulgently at clumsy kids. No accident, Lord, it's a lie—maybe a murderous lie if left unchecked. *Bless neighbors, kin, teachers who notify authorities. Ease their guilt about tattling.*

Guide us through the mire of getting involved, for we worry about disputing parental explanations and rights. Who, we fret, dares risk ruining reputations, businesses, relationships? We all must dare when we suspect. *Give us courage to intervene, and strength to build and support an equitable, strong system, even as we grieve its necessity and effectiveness.*

Lord of peace and gentleness, help us to believe what is plainly before us: Children aren't safe. That said, what an indictment of us if we walk away. Our apathy is as telltale a confession as any marks on X-ray film.

Words of Light

Jesus said, "No more of this!" (Luke 22:51, RSV)

Blue Bike

(In honor of a grown-up child no longer afraid)

Soiled, stained, silenced,
she dried her tears and pedaled home
carrying his secret between her legs and
in her blue bicycle basket.
Soiled, stained, silenced,
she swallowed betrayal like lemon lollipops and
sunshafts stroking the dead yellow kitty he put
in her blue bicycle basket.
Its childhood, too, suddenly ended
in the opening of his zipper, the snapping of a neck
as sacrifice to her silence, guaranteeing
she'd not venture beyond her blue bicycle basket.
Soiled, stained, silenced over years,
yet defiantly coaxing her words
to free-fall tumble beyond his range
and escape with the blue bicycle basket.
Sudsy daylight words rinse away dank silence;
soft hands of counsel brace her voice,
retrieving childhood in whispers, telling
about the burden in the blue bicycle basket.
Sluicing tears flush soil from her body
until all that is left is a brief tilt to her neck
when face to face with yellow tabbies or dust kitties
needing to be cleaned from a blue bicycle basket.
Soiled, stained, silenced no more with his secret,
she carries it in her blue bicycle basket to dump
in his lap with the yellow kitten's bones he'd left her;
turning away, pedaling home, past childhood mended.

Through you, O God, a moment of betrayal needn't be a
lifetime of ruin. Mourn with us ways used to ensure silence.

Celebrate with us children who tell anyway. Get the violators.

Words of Light

Fathers, do not provoke your children. . . . For the wrongdoer will be paid back for the wrong he has done, and there is no partiality. (Colossians 3:21,25, RSV)

Broken Twigs, Broken Promises

Group therapy with children. The words, Lord who called such little ones to your knee, are a contradiction in terms. Surely they have no need, for there are no bruises, casts, or crutches, no wounds. At least none are visible. *Give us eyes to see beyond the surface.*

Listen to their conversations, though. Watch their play and admire their drawings, and the wounds are there. Misused kids have calluses on their feelings tougher than a ditchdigger's palms. Let no pain in; let no pain out. *O God, can they ever be baby-soft again? Heal these hidden wounds.*

Even playing, they're sharing secrets from the mole burrows of fear where they live. They have a game, "Feels Like This Color." What color is sad? Sad is brown, the color of Daddy's belt. Sad is hot pink, the color of Mommy's shredding fingernails. Sad is white, the color of Daddy's underwear when he plays "Secret." Sad is blue, the inside of a closet. "But isn't every color sad?" they wonder, perched like chickadees on the colored squares, waiting for a new answer. *Pass on your healing answers through us. Our sad color can only be a rainbow stitched from all theirs.*

Family portraits line the wall with terrifying metaphors: big scissors dicing, tall knives slicing, tiny stick-people burning, their mouths screaming in blank cartoon captions above their heads. How silent is their cry for help; how grave their danger when they tattle about the slicing and dicing. *Help us to believe them and intervene.* Help them to hold on until help comes. Send us to them, for their two hours of therapy is flimsy protection against their peril.

Words of Light

Jesus wept. (John 11:35, NASB)

Train up a child in the way he should go. (Proverbs 22:6, RSV)

Truth Is Better Than Fiction

Like mice chasing each other through a maze, our thoughts pursue elusive answers, "Why, why, why? Can my memories be true?" *Unbelievable.* Not only do others have trouble believing when we tell of childhood violation, but we doubt our reality, too. *Unbelievable.*

Ease our doubts when we recite from an endless list of *unbelievable* facts that have our faces. Tucked into frozen memory are places and names to whisper to you. This is almost more than we can bear, because it is seldom strangers who do the greatest harm, God of broken hearts. Kin of assorted shapes and connections, baby-sitters, parents' friends, friends of friends, whoever it may be, steal our innocence as they violated our bodies, minds, and spirits. It *is* unbelievable to discover that people we loved and trusted are not only capable of but are skilled in treachery. *Hold us while we wail in disbelief and pain from their atrocities.*

Doubting our own reality also makes faith in you a casualty: How could a loving parent let something like this happen? This is perhaps the most unbelievable. *Accept the only prayer we have right now: our confusion and hesitation to trust even you.* In your hands, where we leave this prayer, it can be redeemed into assurance that violence, evil are never your intention.

Our belief that what we *say* happened *did* happen is first step in recovery; how hard this is, Lord. We can deal with others' doubts later. So often families paint themselves into such normal-looking portraits that as children we couldn't dispute the lies. Now we are grown-up big— bigger than family secrets, intimidation.

Help us to understand that acceptance of fact is as much a state of mind and heart as it is of evidence: Even with eyewitnesses, we struggle to accept the truth that someone targeted us for vileness. Like ghosts who refuse to stay buried, memories of the violator rise again. They demand our attention, so we can lay them, at last, to true rest. *Keep us steadfast in the face of challenge, our own and others.*

With your support, we will believe the unbelievable and speak the unspeakable as part of your healing ways, knowing "the truth will set us free" (John 8:32 NIV). As we do, we cling to an even greater truth: We are your loved children, believed and comforted, despite others' efforts to harm and distort reality.

Help us to believe we can find value in a life contaminated by others' treachery. Assure us that the freedom and comfort gained is equal to the pain of truth, a life-giving equation.

Words of Light

Lord, when doubts fill my mind, . . . quiet me. (Psalm 94:19, TLB)

Paper Chains

Link to link, God of caring circles, we connect events in our lives like colored strips to create a paper chain. With trembling hands, we also include vile events that touched us, affecting who we are today. Those are the ripped, torn scraps of paper that, through your guidance, we patched into the chain.

We are becoming tolerant of those patched places where we fixed leftover damage. Symptoms of isolation, fear; not being able to play, relax, trust, excel; and habits and behaviors that limit us, although they once actually saved our lives. We are grateful that we paid attention, tended these patches, and replaced them with better tools for coping. We add the new tools to our chain, for they connect us to healing's rounded wholeness.

Today is a new link, the color of hope. We believe it is you holding the ends of the chain of events, forging past to present to future, strengthening, lengthening the chain. The patches are becoming just part of the events of our lives. In your hands, the torn scraps and most tattered souls heal together again to make, like our paper chain, a garland to hang on the grandest holiday tree.

Words of Light

Behold, I am making all things new. (Revelation 21:5, NASB).

What Do You Feed a Nightmare?

Black and white or Technicolor, dreams are leading us closer to promised recovery as they link memory to reality. Stay close, O God, when they become nightmares filled with familiar pursuers and recollected violence.

Monsters lurk beneath our beds, even though we are no longer little kids. We *know* monsters are there, for they always were; the nightmares were real. Shine your light beneath our beds and into our souls' dreaming vastness. Truth and healing are waiting to replace these spots, like our dreams, with new images and truths.

We are trying to be grateful for even nightmarish and terrifying dreams, for they are helping us to recover. Assure us that we wouldn't be dreaming if we weren't strong enough to peek at what they offer. With your arms around us and held in the hands of skillful caregivers, we are safe to remember what our dreams already know.

Remember the old joke about taking hay to bed to feed nightmares? Guide us to provide proper nourishment to this wondrous part of ourselves, which you created to be our friend and guide. Not hay, Lord, but love. We'll feed our nightmares love as we tame them to ride into monster-free futures, sleeping and waking.

We feel you leading us as we ride on the backs of our nightmares—originals and reruns—into sunshine no darkness can abide.

Words of Light

I will lie down in peace and sleep, for . . . you will keep me safe. (Psalm 4:8, TLB)

Teach Me To Pray

(For adult children who are remembering)

For years, truth waited. Now through your grace and others' skills, healing is in sight. Anger is stuck, though, like fish bones in the throat. Spluttering in fury, we need to get them out, Lord, so we can go on. Even as we rant and rave, we feel comfort in your unflinching acceptance of us and the words you add to ours.

Hear us as we pray for those who
. . . didn't believe when we told
Have mercy on them.
. . . knew and didn't protect
Have mercy on them.
. . . acted as silent partners and colluders
Have mercy on them.
. . . prayed instead of acted
Have mercy on them.
. . . punished us for telling
Have mercy on them.
. . . trivialize and think it's over because time has merely passed
Have mercy on them.
. . . can't face their own wounds and therefore turn from ours
Have mercy on them.
. . . betray again: from therapists to churches, police to courts
Have mercy on them.
Amen.

Words of Light

In my trouble I cried to the LORD, And he answered me. (Psalm 120:1, NASB)

Scavengers of Hope

B does not necessarily follow *A* in the alphabet of hope when you are the author of our lives. Growing up, O God, in twisted homes does not inevitably make us twisted.

Like Hansel and Gretel in childhood tales, we scavengers of hope are picking up crumbs and pebbles to find our way. We are grateful for the surrogates and stand-ins who left them for us to follow when our own families failed. We are down-on-our-knees grateful for a chance to be different from our families, sad as we are about needing to.

In the face of that need, you, O God, are the ultimate intervener, the great interrupter. For some of us, hope came through our early awareness that we deserved better, were different, were not at fault. For some, hope was relatives, a story overheard, a movie, a book, or a line in a play that provided a "light bulb" of discovery. For some, hope was a kind word from a teacher; praise and encouragement from a relative, even a stranger. You are not limited in whom you use to rescue us. Your chosen ones tell us that we matter and have a choice to live differently, so we can resolve not to twist others' lives, not to treat others as cruelly as we were treated, not to do unto others as was done unto us.

We are grateful that you fortified us for breaking away and following a different path. With your support, we can stop the buck right here and now, and not let past violence run through us like oil through a pipeline. Instead we can stop the meanness and send it back where it started.

Be with us as we follow the path laid for us by those who care. Help us to recognize a pebble or a crumb of hope when we see it, no matter how mundane. Inspiration is like pollen extracted by a bee, small to the eye but enormous in potential.

Help us to continue to rise above cruel pasts to build

accomplished lives filled with healthy relationships. As we do, we will keep a handful of pebbles in our pockets to leave for others who need a path to follow. Love begets love far longer than evil begets evil.

Words of Light

The night is nearly over. (Romans 13:12, NIV)

A Looking-Back Lament

(Based on Psalm 91)

He that dwelleth in the secret place of the most High shall abide under the shadow of the Almighty (Psalm 91:1, KJV).

Shadows are where I dwell and secrets what I still do best.

Others' misuse banished me to a desert of repression and fear;

no Almighty was neighbor in the barren wasteland of my youth.

I will say of the Lord, he is my refuge and my fortress: my God; in him will I trust (v. 2).

Your fortress crumbled, burying me in the rubble of my trust.

I had no refuge when childhood innocence was stolen, hope betrayed.

Why were you not near in that violation of body and soul?

Faith and trust lie crumbled in the dust of flimsy promises.

He will deliver thee from the snare, . . . cover thee with his feathers, and under his wings shalt thou trust: his trust shall be thy shield and buckler (vv. 3,4).

I crouched behind your shield and waited to escape on your wings.

Someone else came, plucking me from safety like a mouse in a field.

I am still snared in that evil will and smothered by the violence.

Trust?

I did, but I got a fistful of betrayal like tail feathers of a vanishing bird.

Thou shalt not be afraid for the terror by night; nor for the

*arrow that flieth by day; nor for the pestilence that walketh
in darkness; . . . A thousand shall fall at thy side and ten
thousand at thy right hand; but it shall not come nigh thee*
(vv. 5-7).

Oh, but it did, God of promises, both night and day.

I am still pursued by arrows of terror, arrows of memory
and shame.

Skepticism and disbelief impale me. Grief blots out the
noonday sun.

Count me among the tens of thousands of innocents still
falling.

*Only with thine eyes shalt thou behold and see the re-
ward of the wicked* (v. 8).

They get off scot free, that's what I see.

See through my eyes their hypocrisy, their triumph.

See through my eyes families who protect images and
kin, not kids.

See battered mates who keep quiet even though it kills
them.

See churches that shield fondlers and rapists behind
faux forgiveness.

See through my eyes victims hunting for answers to
"why?" through booze, pills, food, sex, loneliness, and self-
destruction.

See through my eyes your church silencing and ignoring
me and my sisters and brothers who dwell in another secret place: survivors' hell.

Words of Light

(Psalm 91)

To Our Violators:
What We Wish for You

I bring no prayer today, Hearer of silent pleas, for my
rage and hatred are not fit to say aloud. I want my violator
in hell with the lid clamped on. Tight. I want my violator
to suffer as I have, my life interrupted, my sleep tor-
mented, fear stalking me like a spider on the back of my
neck.

Fear, rage, and grief demand their turn. Can they be
my prayer? O God, accept my bitterness and hear between
these lines a prayer for healing, healing to the reality of
what happened to me, healing to the possibility that I can
be restored despite it, healing of the hatred and bitterness
that tie me to the past. Be with me as I confront my violator:

*I wish you to suffer physical, mental, and spiritual disas-
ter.* (I confess this is not a rational or nice prayer, but, O
God, how I sometimes wish it.)

I want you to be punished, justice served.

I want you to be sorry—truly sorry, not just sorry in words.

I want answers: Why me? Why did you pick on me to
vent your sin? Do you care that I am wounded? that I have
nightmares you caused? How did you justify the unequal
balance of power? I was a kid.

How do you feel now? You seem so untouched and nor-
mal.

I feel you with me, great Healer, as I find new words for
my enemy:

*I want to be able to value myself, since you didn't. I want
to go on without hating you. I want compassion for your
pitiful life, no matter how successful you appear. I want to
forgive you so I can be freed from you.*

I want what I already have: a new life, courage to enjoy
it, a heart that can learn forgiveness. I have so much to

look forward to that there is no longer much reason to look behind me, where I am leaving you.

Amen and Amen.

Words of Light

Pour out your wrath on them; . . . May their place be deserted; . . . Charge them with crime upon crime; . . . May they be blotted out of the book of life. . . . (Psalm 69:24-28, NIV)

How to Explain

It's difficult to explain, Lord, why we don't go home for Christmas or celebrate birthdays with family. But you and we know that they were *family* in name and outward appearance only, that the deeper scenes were not for public consumption. We grieve again at that reality, even as we are down-on-our-knees grateful that we have moved mind, body, and soul from its darkness.

But it's hardest at family times to allow others to live the consequences of *their* actions. We are sad on their behalf, even as we wonder if they really mourn us or are just annoyed at our escape. Give us broad shoulders to hold the anger and blame they heap upon us for not accepting *their* responsibility. It's tempting to give in, to give in to the pressure to pretend, but giving in would be going back into the danger and darkness we've left. Help us through this yearning moment.

When we are lonely, remind us that loneliness is the small price we pay for being okay, safe, and becoming healed. When relatives are angry at our desertion, remind us that we can't expect applause for disturbing the images on the family portrait. Hold us as we mourn for what we wish had been around that family table. Sadly, Lord, it is being gone from that table that we celebrate.

Keep those we left in the hollow of your hand; be ready in case hearts open, behaviors change. In the meantime, join us at lonely holidays and family events, reassuring us that our strength is your joy.

Words of Light

The joy of the LORD is your strength. (Nehemiah 8:10, NIV)

Generation to Generation

Like David against Goliath, Miriam against Pharaoh, we outsmarted the forces of darkness that stalked us. As children in toxic homes, the odds were not in our favor, the chances of success slim, if we are to believe such things. But we believed *beyond* that, O God, our hope in ages past and in years to come. We believed that we did not have to be abusers as we were abused. We believed we did not have to be violent and mean-spirited, as others were to us. We believed your love for us was stronger than the meanness we were taught.

Use our shaky roots and faulty foundations as something upon which to build, just as you built upon Peter and Mary Magdalene and Paul and the others. We read with increasing joy and awe how you repeatedly intervened. What joy to live in that hope.

We are grateful for your presence, which led them and us to become more than the scripts we were dealt. It is answered prayer that led us to your redeeming, refining knee, where we are becoming so much more than the sum of heredity, environment, and the nasty ways we were treated. Join us in a triumphant christening of a new us. The sound of something breaking is not a champagne bottle shattering over a hull, but rather the cycle of violence shattering, ending with us. As your son said, "Enough!"

Words of Light

And hope does not disappoint us. (Romans 5:5, NASB)

Burning Buildings

We recall the violence we escaped and shiver at the close call. Thank you for empowering us to escape. Yet, God, beneath whose sheltering wings we are recovering, safety is a two-edged blessing: We had to leave others behind, as if we were abandoning them in a burning building.

We agonized over options, even as we accepted the choice: leave or perish. How can we live with ourselves, though, when we look over our shoulders and see those still stuck in darknesses we left: violent homes, abusive families, battering relationships, toxic workplaces, sinister neighborhoods. What is our responsibility to those left behind? O God of new beginnings, help us to make peace with our guilt from surviving, so we can build something useful from this fresh start.

Where we *can* make a difference, fortify us to stay for the duration and to be inspired, energetic advocates for change.

Where we *cannot* make a difference and become part of the problem when we agitate for unwanted change, help us to shake the dust from our feet and move out the door to your promised abundant life. Help us to understand that we are not quitters but rather sensible stewards of our lives.

Be with those left behind, Lord, even if we can't be. Inspire them if the time comes to take heart from our exit. Show them our footprints leading away, so that they may follow; show them our hands outstretched in support.

Thank you for your footprints, which we are now following. Life is too precious to waste in burning buildings.

Words of Light

When doubt fills my mind, . . . quiet me. (Psalm 94:19, TLB)

The Power of Violence

Committee Member

Save me a seat on the "heavenly judgment committee," God of final reckonings. I have names to submit and punishments to recommend.

I'm only half joking, but the way things are, we want to believe in judgment, some eternal, cosmic justice. *Guide us to leave it to you.*

In the meantime, the dreadful wrongs that go unpunished torment us, and we call to you in frustration and grief. Step in, O God of great armies and tumbling Jericho walls, and bring down those who spray bullets in classrooms, who rape and rob old women, who torture children and pets.

No need for me to go on, O God, because you know it all and weep first.

How can we accept violators' "getting away with it"? How can we tolerate evildoers who receive light or suspended sentences for deeds done when "temporarily insane"? or who wield money and power enough to get off?

No joke, Lord, we want retribution, equalized evil.

We do not want to hear, "Judge not." We do not want to relinquish control of consequences. We do not want to forgive. We do not want to be rational, civilized. We do not want to be patient, to work within the system.

No, we are frustrated with the system, furious at successful evildoers, and we want tangible, satisfying consequences, if not Here, then There.

We apologize that a weary cynicism is our only prayer right now. Hold and comfort us, O God, until we can see clearly, feel renewed. Until then, protect us from ourselves: How easy it is to yearn to be cosmic bill collectors and to miss the rest of our here-and-now lives.

Words of Light

Who are you that you judge your neighbor? (James 4:12, RSV)

Compounded Betrayal

Violence begets violence, especially in official hands. To say, God of justice, that our system of law and protection is flawed is an understatement. The violated are reinjured when proof of innocence is made theirs, and revioleted when sentiment is unofficially but effectively on the side of perpetrators who "walk."

Working through the system to find justice and resolution feels as if we were weighted punch toys that, when knocked down, pop back up to be hit again, again: Restraining orders look good on paper, but they are as useless as spit wads in the hands of those who don't enforce them. Rapists, molesters, and batterers plea-bargain back into our daily lives to stalk and strike. (The average prison sentence for men who kill their female partners is two to six years.) Children who tell are returned to unsafe homes in the name of "family." Professionals are burned out, cynical.

The list is as long as a clogged court docket.

Sad, sad, Lord. Is it any wonder that we, victim and advocate, are torn between *depression* and *vigilantism?* Are these the options Justice holds on her scales? Revive us, God of hope, and goad us to work for reform, to monitor prosecutors' records and judges' convictions, to legislate change, to be advocates. Fortify us when violence is done to us, so we will settle for nothing less than justice. Equip us to reject justice's attempt to elude us.

It's bad enough that we can't walk our streets, play unmolested as youth, and be safe, if not cherished, in our marriages. But we know the system is waiting to shout "Gotcha!"

Words of Light

You have always cared for me in my distress; now hear me as I call again. (Psalm 4:1, TLB)

Blaming the Victim

See the coon on the highway? Lord. Poor thing, a hit and
run victim. Watch with us in horror as folks back up and
run over it again. Hold your hands over our ears to shut
out their "Gotcha" satisfaction at further ruining one of
your creatures.

We are those broken creatures left alongside the high-
ways of life, victims of random mugging, rape, family
meanness, childhood trauma. Then, *boom,* we are
slammed again by attitudes and a system that insists we
caused our own violation.

The very idea is obscene.

Things must change, renewing God: The tail is wagging
the dog as the lawless break, mock, and use the law to escape accountability by turning the spotlight on victims to
be blamed.

Blaming victims has long been popular sport, dear God,
with jokes made about rape victims secretly enjoying it,
theft victims really pulling insurance scams, and incest victims lying to settle old scores. *Make them stop their lies.
Enough.*

To claim to be a "victim" is to invite harassment and
trial by innuendo. We grieve to see a backlash rising
against those who act differently, who believe, advocate,
support. We grieve that too often "extenuating circumstances" are used to barter for violators' freedom. Violators
get sympathy and leniency, while victims get scrutiny and
challenge. Not fair, not fair, Lord of righteous anger.

Chastise those who point at victims' pain or ignorance.
Require better behavior from those charged to uphold and
administer law. Teach them to respect others' pain and
grief. *We* could teach them how, Lord, by turning the tables
so those who judge *us* would be in *our* shoes. Imagine the
howls of indignation! Teach them compassion any way you

can, Lord, our way or yours. And reprimand those who excuse violators. Don't they realize *their* children, homes, or bodies could be next?

Send us believers and advocates who, like us, will not be intimidated by bullies on the first, second, or third try. Stand with us in courts of law when we proceed *as if* justice is possible. Someone has to respect its promise.

Stand with us when we begin to doubt ourselves, worrying, "If only." "If only I'd dressed, talked, walked, driven, locked up differently, I could've prevented what happened." "I shouldn't have married him/her." "I asked for it, deserved what I got." Nonsense, teach us to say, to pray.

Keep us strong. If we become too jaded to speak and act, then our violators are right: Truth can be manipulated and justice mocked. No way, no way. Help us, O God, to hold onto truth so tenaciously that no one can pull it from our grasp. No one can make a loophole through which to escape the truth that we neither cause our violation nor accept that insinuation. Set your seal upon that truth. It's where we stake our lives.

Words of Light

Insults have broken my heart. . . . I looked for pity, but there was none; and for comforters, but I found none. (Psalm 69:20, RSV)

Too High a Ransom to Pay

If it hasn't happened yet, O God, we fear, no, we are sure, it will: We will become victims of violence. Big or little, random or selected, violation is coming our way. Be with us on the edge of our seats where we hold ourselves hostage to fear.

Daily vigilance is wearing us out: Where should we park the car? Should we get in the elevator? answer the door even to kin, most violent of all? smile at neighbor, stranger? The gap between worry and paranoia is not as clear as it was in a once-upon-a-gentler time. Suspicion, Lord—someone is up to no good—is often right on the mark.

Although we pay the high price of lost joy and freedom as ransom for being hostages to fear, we're still not free. We even cheat ourselves of you, treating you as a cosmic rabbit's foot to protect us from harm, then discarding you when violence strikes. You are so much more dependable than this, Creator God. You are a resource to help us to be courageous and creative when taking back our streets, our towns, our nights, our days, our joy.

Help us to bear the personal consequences of communal problems. Form us into neighborhood watch groups. Support us as we boycott products, programs, and producers of things that glorify hate. Send us as advocates for those like the elderly, who are imprisoned in neighborhoods, easy prey for roaming evil. Urge us to strengthen the system designed to protect, which falls so short of its goal. Guard us from defeatist cynicism.

Above all, free us from the belief that we are safest when we cower, and remind us that we will not be ransomed by anything less than our own inspired efforts to make a difference ourselves. As we step out in courage, give us a sixth sense to know when to duck the stray bullet. These are uneasy times.

Words of Light

God is . . . always ready to help in times of trouble. So we will not be afraid. . . . (Psalm 46:1-2, GNB)

Killer Instinct

We sit in the bleachers of a violent world, God of play and laughter, cheering violence. We complain when games are civilized, blame sportsmanlike conduct when our team loses. "Chicken!" we shout. "Getting mad might help team get even," headlines advise before a rematch. We boo friendly rivalry, preferring down-and-dirty playing, and pay megabucks to those who do. We eat, drink, watch, wear, and yes, believe what they endorse.

Do we dare consider that there might be a link between the playing field and off-the-field violence? Let's do an instant replay of our own lives: Are we affected by these meaner and win-at-all-costs standards? Do play and sport serve as models for the way we relate at home and work? Do we then demand to be exempt from the consequences of playing dirty? bullying? tantrums?

O God, forgive us, player and fan, when violent, win-at-all-costs attitudes extend past sports arenas and locker rooms into homes and relationships. Listen as our kids play the game they call "Kill the Man That's Got It." Pounding, dragging, and screaming at one another over a ball on the playground, they are playing versions of our favorite sports. The common denominator is a desire not just to defeat but to destroy.

Help us to ponder why sportsmanlike conduct is a relic of the past, why "killer instinct" is a sought-after quality, why we make heroes out of off-the-field convicted batterers and abusers. In the heat of the contest and at the heart of these questions, help us, God of fair play, to restore joy to the game on field and off.

Words of Light

I will try to walk a blameless path, but how I need your help, especially in my own home, where I long to act as I should. (Psalm 101:2, TLB)

Signs of the Times

If seeing is believing, God of love, hate is fashionable. Check out our T-shirt messages—"Kill," "Stomp," and "_____," or "_____" —suggestions, quotes, and pictures to offend any race, creed, gender, or taste. We pray lightly and with humor here because we're tired of complaining. We're also more than a little afraid of those whose meanness might be more than shirt deep. So, we confess, we laugh.

From T-shirts and hats to bumper stickers and billboards, anger is so popular that we wear it! Signs of the times. *"My God can beat up your God"* has to be my favorite. Is it true?! Heaven help us, even faith can be used to slap people around, to annoy, divide, separate, dominate.

Shirts with a message *are* fun, and we welcome like-shirted folks who share our concerns. Some of the naughty ones, well, we may smile a little as we shake our heads. But there is a rock in the snowball of free expression, Lord: Hate is still hate, no matter how well it rhymes or what cause it claims. Even shirts that proclaim "love" cover souls that betray the message!

We need to pay attention to beliefs that others put on a shirt or a car. Even hate, maybe *especially* hate. Open our eyes, Lord, to the wearers' needs as we read their loathsome messages. Give us patience, compassion, and energy to combat the reasons they wrote them.

Words of Light

You must be a new and different person . . . Clothe yourself in this new nature. . . . Say only what is good and helpful to those you are talking to, and what will give them a blessing. (Ephesians 4:24,29, TLB)

In the Audience

We, O God, love the adventure sandwiched between television commercials, and we thrill at pursuits, captures, and terminations in the movies and videos we watch, the books we read, the songs we dance to, the games we play.

What an appetite we have for violence that tickles and titillates.

We confess we enjoy lounging on our couches, tilt-back chairs, or padded movie theater seats and vicariously doing away with one another to the glare of the tube, the blare of the CD, the light of the blood-silvered screen.

What is wrong with this picture, Lord?

Is it the passive stance we take, propped up and reclining, waiting to be spoonfed violence and thrills? Is it our insatiable appetite for excitement that we try to satisfy with harsh, empty scenes and rat-a-tat plots? Is it our leftover, wired, jaded feelings once the entertainment is done? Is it our hunger for bigger, faster, crashier scenes, each one wilder than the last?

What's wrong with this picture? Something, we suspect, for when we look, we see life is imitating art *and* the other way around; either way, it's violent. Lead us to answers, for we are uneasy in our easy chairs. We are vaguely concerned that we can tolerate so much gore and mayhem.

What's wrong with this picture? Who we become: When we're empty receptacles to be filled with adrenaline-pumping, by-standing adventure, we turn off, numbing ourselves to the real violence that needs our attention.

Unplug us, Creator of choices, so we can tell the difference between real and make-believe pain. We've been remotely controlled long enough.

Words of Light

As he thinks within himself, so he is. (Proverbs 23:7, NASB)

Numb to Violence

What we see, read, hear, and sing along to, dear God, has numbed us like Novocaine in a jaw. We can't feel the drilling of our own sensitivities or hear the cries of those who need us. We are shockproof from an overload of violence and doomsayers.

With our callused attitudes, we are ashamed to stand before you, the God who is moved by the plight of the smallest sparrow. *Help us to soften and bend; forgive our inattention.*

We are overwhelmed by what's going awry, backlashes included. If provoked for an opinion at all, we vote for slick solutions to problems that, like a junkyard dog, are going to circle around and bite us on the hindsight side. *Reenergize us; wake us up.*

We are cheating ourselves of feelings, feelings that might be scary when we look at the world we tune out. Feelings that could lead us to take action, plot interventions, and offer hands-on assistance. Feelings that are authentic, not synthetic substitutes for the real thing, painful as they might be.

Violence-overload is no excuse for dropping out, numbing, dumbing down, but, O God, it's the only prayer we can think to offer this minute. We think we simply can't handle any more news. But, finally, we know we can do better. We will unplug our ears and listen to what's *really* in the babble and rabble: *You* are asking us to help. It might take a while to get feeling back into souls and minds we've numbed to protect ourselves, but we'll be there.

Words of Light

Be doers of the word, and not hearers only, deceiving yourselves. (James 1:22, NKJV)

Hit with a Punch Line

We deplore the violence around us, but we ignore the lust for it within ourselves. This has been a well-guarded secret, but now we want to share it with you, God who gave all so we might have peace. We are uneasy with how simple getting revenge can be. How much fun.

"You hurt me, I'll hurt you back," we vow. And we can, thanks to 800-number revenge services, clever gifts to send someone who's hurt us, hate toys, and greeting cards reminding "We wish the very worst for you!"

"But, hey, we've been hurt," we protest, and often they do deserve it. Besides, it's just a joke, just humor with a small barb. Lighten up, Lord.

What do you think of us when we send a cactus with a message, "Sit on it?" Send dead roses to loves who've cast us off? Send dead animals? Send a truck load of manure? In the name of getting even, we "aim for the funny bone," as if humor could cover up our smoldering, mean-spirited, albeit socially acceptable, clever violence.

Forgive us, merciful God, when we smile at the humor in revenge; the last laugh may be on us.

Words of Light

Never pay back evil for evil to anyone. (Romans 12:17, NASB)

Self-destruct Button

At the moment of violation, we fought to survive like cornered animals. Why now, O God, are we willing to relinquish our fought-for life in ways that threaten to do what the violator couldn't: destroy us?

Booze, pills, risky sex, risky play, risky driving; food, too much or too little; unchecked depression; suicide attempts by nearly four out of ten battered women, with three out of ten white women and nearly half their African American sisters succeeding. That Jesus suffered does not mean we should imitate his wounds: His suffering was not a desire to self-destruct. To the contrary, he, like we, encountered repellent, uncalled-for evil.

We are grateful that you, loving Parent, led him and now us through suffering. Your joy is the strength of your children. You healed his wounds; now heal ours. Anything else would make you just another abusive parent. We know you instead as God of consolation, renewal, and limitless energy.

Forgive us when we falter. Give us a defiant hope. Hold up a mirror for us to see ourselves wearing, like off-season coats, shame that others—the violators—should wear. It doesn't fit, doesn't look like us, so why should we allow it to determine the shape of our living? Take it away, God of new seasons.

In your grace-full redemption, we soon will run coatless through days when thought of harming ourselves is just a memory, like an abyss into which someone *else* tried to push us. Instead we grabbed your hand, determined to scramble back to life in the promise of your healing.

Valiant, Lord, we are valiant, and not even momentary depression or fleeting memory can unloose our hand from yours. That is our promise to you . . . and our answer to your promise.

Words of Light

Do not fear; you are of more value than . . . sparrows.
(Matthew 10:31, NASB)

Blessed is the man who trusts in the LORD, ... He is like a
tree planted by water, that sends out roots by the stream
and does not fear when heat comes, for its leaves remain
green, and is not anxious in the year of drought. (Jeremiah
17:7-8, RSV)

Drive-by Shoutings

Shouldn't there be disclaimers, God of discernment, at the beginning of the drive-by shoutings that pass for talk shows and commentaries: "I'm doing this so you will buy my book, video, products." Or, "Elect me!"

Fanning hatred for fame and fortune is big business these days, and we give little thought, if any, to the cost we pay for their agitation. Encourage us to look behind rhetoric to motive before we follow, write a check. Is it a lust for money and power? Are they the tempters you've cautioned us about before?

And speaking of bucks, peace-loving God, the shouters, proclaimers, inciters, shredders of dialogue pass the buck of responsibility when their advice, "Hate," is taken. They accept no role when their advice ignites or supports extreme actions. Chastise them, Lord, and let them have the decency to stop the buck of subsequent violence where it belongs: in their hands, as unclean as their mouths.

Oh, to be sure, commentators who play with words of fire do not cause violence, any more than music lyrics cause rampant sex or cop killings. But Lord, hotheaded talkers—political to religious—do legitimize violence. Bombers, bashers, and bigots hear their words as permission, invitation, blessing to go and do as instructed: hate.

Drive-by shoutings destroy hope, peace, fairness, and trust as effectively as drive-by shootings strike down elderly folks waiting at a bus stop or kids going into a day-care center. Hate kills one way or another.

Give us good sense, O God, not to listen, watch, buy, repeat, believe, support, tolerate, or ignore hate in any form— syndicated, deified, elected, or top of the charts.

Words of Light

Let no one deceive you with empty words. (Ephesians 5:6, NASB)

A chattering fool comes to ruin. . . . The mouth of the righteous is a fountain of life, but violence overwhelms the mouth of the wicked. Hatred stirs up dissension, but love covers all wrongs. (Proverbs 10:10-12, NIV)

Bang! You're Dead

God, our fortress, which is best: pepper mace or high-pitched alarms? And what brand gun should we use? We're afraid to venture far without an answer—and expertise in and commitment to using our weapon of choice.

Armed and ready, we go to work, doze in our recliners, and walk the dog. Armed and ready, we wait for the first hint of attack. *Help us to be correct when we spot it. Too many "intruders" we shoot turn out to be a relative, a neighbor, a family pet.*

On the one hand, we have the right to carry weapons, bear arms, defend ourselves—a right worth protecting. On the other, how are we to reconcile learning self-defense with talking about peacemaking? Arming ourselves with turning the other cheek? How can we speak love but approve capital punishment, the ultimate self-defense? *Help us to consider whether we would be willing to pull the switch, inject a lethal dose, before we approve it. There are times, Lord, there are times, when it would be easy. Guide us here.*

Complexity in an issue we want to keep simple is troubling, for we are angry that we feel afraid in our homes, communities. Do you want us to take up arms against one another, no matter how many innocent get caught in the crossfire? And what about those who see peace as the greatest enemy and who think defeat lies in negotiation? Sometimes, Lord, we think we should arm ourselves against them! Are we about to wage civil war?

Help us to figure out how to take sensible precautions, while we ponder what it means to be armed peacemakers.

Words of Light

Be angry, and yet do not sin. (Ephesians 4:26, NASB)

Herded by Hatred

Violence against us is never our doing, God of blessed diversity, and it is never fair. Yet, it is more maddeningly unfair when entire groups of us are herded and hunted for being us.

As a culture, gender, caste, denomination, neighborhood, race, age, we are battered and defiled as a clot, a clump, a group, not individuals at all. This stripping away of our self-ness, Lord, is terrifying and familiar, recalling "cleansings" that reverberate through headlines even today.

The sin of generalization, God, is a timeless favorite. Refined for our world, it condemns *all* women as militant challengers for power they don't deserve; *all* men as potential rapists, chauvinists, withholders of power; *all* teens as gang members and dropouts; *all* bosses as unfair in hirings and firings. A list of generalizations to justify violence goes on and on, without even mentioning color, creed, sexual preference, lifestyle, and appearance.

We are beaten down by the sheer force of blind, unthinking group hatred. It's difficult to feel hopeful about solutions that begin with one-to-one healings and personal conversions. Fat chance, Lord, fat chance. The chorus of hating voices is growing more shrill as it gains heady power, from political platform to pulpit, where hate crimes are defended as necessary to "purify society." Help us to stand firm in the face of such armored-tank-like violence. Remind us to hold hands and gain strength from one another's unique abilities to oppose.

Help us to see even the enemy as a "one" to be reached, gentled. Give us tools for one-to-one assessment and face-to-face negotiation.

Words of Light

The one who guards his mouth preserves his life; The one

who opens wide his lips comes to ruin. . . . The companion of fools will suffer harm. (Proverbs 13:3,20, NASB)

Excuse Me

The list of excuses for meanness, God of truth, stretches from here to there: family, society, culture, stress, media, too much work, too little work. Violators whine, blame, and claim provocation and weak-mindedness. Even your legendary adversary gets in the excuse-me act: "The devil made me do it."

Perhaps.

Nothing can excuse violating. Explain, yes, but not excuse. Remind us about free will and that we choose our responses to the hands we are dealt. Remind us that each choice brings consequences only we own. Lead us to understand that excusing is not the same as forgiving, which requires accountability and facing truths. In your wisdom, God, you created forgiveness as an intricate process: we have to face facts in order to be healed and to be able to forgive, and violators have to face facts in order to be forgiven and perhaps change.

We are weary of legal shenanigans that legitimize excuses and let bullies slip through loopholes. Help us to protest this, for even legally "excusing" violators of their responsibility ambushes victims again. Excusing, accepting that there are good reasons for violence, also makes us partners in crime. No way, Lord, no way.

Teach us tough compassion.

Words of Light

"Do you want to be healed?" (John 5:6, RSV)

Monkey See, Monkey Do?

God of Solomon, bring your wisdom to our debate: If monkey sees, will monkey do? If our kids play violence, will they seek its reality? If they sing about bashing, will they bash? If they watch porn, will they substitute its rush for committed couplings? If they watch 8,000 murders and 100,000 other acts of violence by the time they are in junior high school, will they . . . we don't know what! Does monkey have to do what monkey sees?

We are as violently divided over the answer as the question, Lord, for we fear censorship and banning as much as we do any presumed effect. At the heart of it, the generation hot on our heels is scared and scary. Can we stop the epidemic of violence by gentling the kids?

Help us to start this gentling by respecting kids. Cartoons, kiddy shows, movies and videos, commercials are often filled with cynical, sarcastic asides and double meanings to hook adolescents and adults. Scold the shameful stewards of children's innocence, O God, which they corrupt at the drop of a coin.

If thought is deed, where, God of both, is the line between play and performance? the link between entertainment and action? the restraining balance between pretend and preparation?

We buy toy arsenals, war and computer annihilation simulations, and call it play, only to wonder why kids so quickly choose "termination" to solve problems, why a quarter million of them take handguns to school. We set killing, disrespect, and assault to catchy tunes, Lord, and wonder why streets are unsafe, kids are killed, and killers succeed in the greatest numbers ever. (A child growing up in our country is fifteen times as likely to be killed by gunfire as a child in Northern Ireland!) We spread rape, torture, degradation, and terror from screen to shining screen and wonder why little boys grow up to batter and one in five little girls grows up to be raped.

One part of this is easy, Lord: chastise our indulgence of kids who whine to see and hear what we know they shouldn't. Help us to turn around *our* failure to establish safe boundaries. No wonder kids don't feel safe: We let in all monsters imaginable! At the same time, keep us from overreacting and tossing out the baby with the bath water in fits of censorship and fear!

Where is the connection between thought and deed? In the hands of parents and adults, in *our* hands, O God. *Our* lack of guidance, we admit with shame, blurs the lines between pretend and reality. *Our* use of screen and jammin' stereo substitutes for talking and relating. Kids learn choices from us: first, how to understand what they see, hear, and do in play; second, whether to go and do likewise.

Likely, God, children will do what we do and say. Make us worthy of the scrutiny.

Words of Light

For as he thinketh in his heart, so is he. (Proverbs 23:7, KJV)

It would be better for him if a millstone were hung around his neck and he were thrown into the sea, than that he cause one of these little ones to stumble. (Luke 17:2, NASB)

Silence Counts

Silence counts in deafening ways, listening Lord. It speaks eloquently of our unwillingness to get involved, to make humane connections between ourselves and others. Yet who can blame us for keeping distance, staying out of trouble, minding our own business?

As usual in our choose-up-sides world, it isn't that simple. We worry while watching late, late news: Is our passivity contributing to communal, global, and corporate violence? fueling its wrath?

But, listen up, Lord! It doesn't concern me! How could it? If a war or conflict is going on where I don't have to see its muddy, bloody streams running past my doorway, if I can't hear its thudding dull explosions and weeping lost children, am I responsible? If my house isn't torched in racial attacks; if my child isn't kidnapped, molested; if I don't bash lesbians and gays or the homeless; if I don't harass and rape, stalk kids, or kick puppies, am I equally indicted alongside whose who do, because I stand silent?

O God, can violence be my silence?

Be with me as I confess to silent evil, for I know in my heart that if I stand in denying silence before concentration camp memory; if I don't weep for women mutilated and raped as spoils of a distant war; if I don't speak by my presence or at least my wallet on issues that don't live in my neighborhood; if I don't legislate, advocate, monitor at-risk children, I am silently endorsing the evil done to all of them.

I, then, am a partner in crime, dear God, a partner in crime. Forgive me and help me to recover my voice and my kinship with all your people, not just those whose names I know.

Words of Light

As for you, speak up for the right living that goes along with true Christianity. (Titus 2:1, TLB)

Back at You

My foot hovered above the gas pedal, ready to tromp, after a rude, impatient driver cut me off at the exit. I was within an inch of showing him, O God, just what righteous indignation is when I realized that I'd best concentrate instead on finding an alternate exit. Get you next time, I vowed; or better yet, the cops will; or maybe you'll have a blowout. Serve him right, I seethed.

It never entered my mind that he might be late to pick up a kid, keep a doctor's appointment, *be* a doctor. No, I instantly reacted as if his sole purpose were to infuriate me personally. My response made clear to him what he could do about that.

We send messages in daily, ordinary violence: We play "chicken" on sidewalks with other pedestrians; rudely scold salesfolk just doing a job; harangue overworked waitpersons; and, my God, fume because some insist we be "politically correct" when we pray! Everyone is push, push, pushing on us.

Is this violence, even though there is no bloodshed? It feels like it, and we wait to see who's going to snipe at us next, who's going to challenge our place on the road, in the pew, at the polls, in conversation, on issues. When they do, we are trigger-happy and loaded for bear.

Is bringing back good manners too simplistic a suggestion for a way to eliminate this violence? Let's not scoff until we try simple solutions first. Our sullen manners and "in your face" belligerence, O God, are a trigger's pull away from all-out combat. I've never been as tired as I am now, cruising the world in which I live, move, and fear for my being. Asking you to "ride shotgun" with me hardly seems appropriate, but it's how I feel.

Words of Light

Be angry but do not sin. (Ephesians 4:26, RSV)

A soft answer turns away wrath, but a harsh word stirs up anger. . . . (Proverbs 15:1, RSV)

Weakness in Numbers

God who welcomes all, last night they stomped someone they hated—a lesbian, a minority person, a foreigner, a cop, a "retard," a "sissy," a homeless man. The crowd cheered. Those who rushed to protect were held back by sweaty hands. Those who wanted to rush forward but didn't were held back by cowardice of the sort that led to your son's death on a splintery cross. *Forgive our reluctance to get involved.*

Bigotry and power are still in the hands of mobs; we haven't learned a thing since that Calvary Friday. We still let loud voices and bullies rule. Help us to bring them down. *Forgive our consent by silence.*

You could cure the soul-sickness of bigotry, God of history, by turning the tables on the tormentors: Make them the minority for a while. Make them prey for musk-scented hunters high on the rush of hate and power. Make them try to get jobs, homes, library cards, and insurance, church memberships and Communion, safe passage down pleasant neighborhood streets. Then let's see what they say. *Forgive our hatred of bigots; we must not become those whom we abhor.*

It isn't going to be as simple as having you do it, is it? Peace and acceptance will be at best an uneasy truce; and tolerance, a tantalizing goal just out of reach. *We* are the ones to raise awareness, teach compassion and empathy. *We* are the ones to be advocates and companions on the mob-strewn way. *We* are the Josephs who will have to help carry burdens, risking our own necks in the interventions. *We* are the Samaritans. *We* are the ones who must expose the fear and lust that drive mob leaders to destroy. *Calm our fear and make us crafty, clever, and strong.*

Hate needs a vehicle, and mobs are tailor-made for the job. On a whim of spite and fear, jealousy, self-doubt, and shame, mobs are manipulated and ignited to stomp and annihilate whomever they choose. Politicians love 'em, preachers use 'em, and we become 'em when we relinquish the personal choice you set before us, O God. *Protect us from the seduction of group evil.*

Bigotry and its companion, mob violence, are obscenities, and we are terrified of their power, especially of their sophisticated, literate, and "spiffed-up" packaging. Douse their cross-burning flames, gag their hate-spewing mouths, and open our ears so we can hear between their persuasive lines a boring message of hate, nothing worth following into a stomping circle where we meet you in the faces of your children, our brothers, sisters.

Words of Light

I know that the LORD will maintain the cause of the afflicted. . . . (Psalm 140:12, NASB)

[Jesus said,] "Which of these . . . was neighbor?" . . . And he said, "He who showed mercy. . . ." Then Jesus said to him, "Go and do likewise . . . ." (Luke 10:36-37, NKJV)

Getcha Coming and Going

Zing, zang. Like the recoil of a bow after the arrow is shot, a backlash, O God of fair play, is a sure thing. It's a special kind of violence, one we call "justified" and "only fair." Currently we have backlashes against retirees, minorities, women, teens. Whoever is perceived at the moment as threatening our status quo becomes a target for a backlash. We almost forgot, we also have backlashes against music, books, videos, movies; against concert-listening, poetry-loving liberals; against men; against tree huggers; against church; against even you.

The common thread we draw tight like a noose, Lord, is that these *objects* used to be *subjects* of admiration, yardsticks to measure against. Today's hero/shero is tomorrow's *objet de* scapegoat, the reason for troubles, for causing our discomfort, replacement, downfall.

It's a crazy-making kind of violence, Lord. But simple minds find simple solutions, and when we are threatened, surely ours are the simplest minds in your creation! Fickle and disloyal, we work for freedom, then lash back at those who are free. We lobby and legislate equality and fairness, then lash back against those who arrive at our side as equals. Women who cry "foul" at rape, harassment, and battering gain support, only to face backlash for destroying family, church, society, business. Read that, Lord, as destroying things the way they were!

Kin to blaming the victim, backlash squeezes its victim like a python its prey. We'd best watch out, for such a canny creature doesn't care who it eats! Sooner or later, it'll get around to us all. Not surprisingly then, the backlash against violence is more violence! Toe to toe we stand and fight, *zing, zang.*

Forgive us for hoarding the good things in life. No one relinquishes power easily, and we don't like to share even a microspeck of it. But until we learn to, it's likely, O God, that we'll keep clanging back and forth like a fly stuck on a pendulum, one extreme to the other. *Zing, zang.* In the process, we in the middle are the ones who get our heads banged on both sides.

Words of Light

[He] shall lay both his hands upon the head of the live goat, and confess over him all the iniquities of the people . . . and shall put them upon the head of the goat, and send him away into the wilderness. . . . (Leviticus 16:21-22 RSV)

You should not have gloated over the day . . . of his misfortune; . . . you should not have rejoiced . . . in the day of their ruin. . . . (Obadiah 1:12, RSV)

Leftovers

Why me? O God. Why me?

This question is not as simple as you might think. We need your guidance to help unlock the answers, for, amazingly, we have taken something that doesn't belong to us: the violator's guilt.

Why me, why us, the victims? Why do we carry the shame and guilt of what was done *to* us? See the violators? Many are oblivious to the damage they do. Listen to the perpetrators: Hear plea-bargained freedom. Look at us, the violated: We are imprisoned in shame from their acts against us!

What is wrong with this picture, this soundtrack of violence?

We get confused while figuring out what happened: Did we cause it? Did we invite it by presenting a perfect target for someone's evil to aim at? Did we deserve it? What is the truth here? Are we to blame?

Heaven help us, we think we should pick up guilt and shame that belongs to someone else! Oh no, dear God, it's not ours. Help us to put it back where it belongs: in the violators' hands. No child deserves neglect, molestation; no spouse deserves bloody bones; no man, woman, or child deserves tearing rapes; no jogger deserves the mugger's assault; no vacationing family deserves drive-by bullets; no . . . the list goes on. Recite the bottom line: Victims do not deserve the guilt that follows the act. Say it again.

Restore our perspective. Ignite righteous rage that will remind us to step over the pile of guilt left behind after the violation, as if it were a bag of rancid, oozing, roach-infested garbage someone dropped in our homes. Who would dirty their hands with someone else's garbage? Not us, God forbid, not us.

Words of Light

My feet came close to stumbling; My steps had almost slipped. . . . Then I perceived their end. . . . Thou dost set them into slippery places; . . . Thou wilt guide me. (Psalm 73:2,17-18,24, NASB)

Revenge **Is** *Sweet*

I knew better. I did it anyway: I got revenge.

It was, O God, a wonderfully sweet moment when the plan fell into place and slipped neatly, like cogs in a wheel, into sync with the violence done to me.

Revenge is sweet.

Admit it, Lord, we are justified in wanting revenge after treachery and betrayal. It is satisfying to line up people who've acted violently against us and to make them pay. From that first moment of meanness, we fantasize about how great it will feel to do as has been done unto us. It will be sweet, indeed, to make it happen.

And yet, and yet.

Like cider turned to vinegar, something is happening to the satisfaction. Why this misery in body and depression in soul? Meanness (theirs) and vengeance (ours) is all we focus on. Our hunger for inflicting pain is growing. We have become like hamsters on a treadmill, running faster and faster to keep ahead of acknowledging who we've become: haters. Something has gone dreadfully awry.

We are not created to be mean, loving Parent, are we? Nor did you create us to be easy agents of hate. You gave us instead nagging consciences, guilty feelings, remorse. And it is this misery (thank you, God) that separates us from those who choose to be mean. Do we really want to be no better?

But wait! They must, must not get away with the evil done to us.

Calm our worries, for it is said that you "set them in slippery places" (Psalm 73:18, NASB) and others have prayed that they will be "blotted out of the book of life" (Psalm 69:28, NASB). For us to hang around and make it happen is to risk slipping and blotting ourselves right out of your plan for us!

Reluctantly we pray for strength to leave the sentencing to the courts and final reckonings to you. Give us, O God, courage to live without perhaps ever seeing it happen. Help us to understand that our desire for justice, vindication, and resolution is not the same as getting revenge. *Remind us that letting go of revenge is not the same as acknowledging "defeat."* We are choosing what is best for us. We are choosing to respond to pain differently than violators do.

Revenge is sweet in the heat of the moment. Remind us of the bitter aftertaste. Forgive us a temporary lapse in judgment when we are successful in getting revenge. We fall to our knees and hear you say, "You are forgiven. Go and sin no more." We won't, merciful God. We won't.

Words of Light

Do not take revenge, my friends, but leave room for God's wrath. (Romans 12:19, NIV)

Once Burned, Twice Shy

As wary as a kicked pup, we approach you again, O God. We've brought our anger that you didn't protect us; we're healing from that. We're pondering shades and gradations of forgiveness and will get back to you about that. Ditto, revenge. Fear? Manageable right now. Thank you for your concern. What's left is trust in you: We've lost it.

How can we trust you will answer, much less shelter us? It didn't happen before; why should we trust now? Because you never left us.

It is, we confess, we who are untrustworthy, who have a fickle faith that assumes you aren't around when life isn't peaceful and safe. Forgive us for thinking that our own violation—and any in our world—is your intention. Loss of trust comes when we assume that you are present, companion Lord, only in good times. Our kind of trust attributes "bruises" to you and assumes you did this to us by allowing it to happen.

Help us to overhaul our paltry trust and make it a stubborn trust that assumes you are always with us; that when we are violated, your heart breaks first. We trust you to be in the redemption of the knife-point rape. We trust you to be in the healing of the mugged victim's wounds, in the abused child forgiving and moving on beyond molesting parent.

We trust you to be at the center of our healing. We trust you to be wherever we are, a constant, reliable, steadfast companion.

Words of Light

On the day I called, thou didst answer me; Thou didst make me bold with strength in my soul. (Psalm 138:3, NASB)

Let Bygones Be Bygones

The deed is done. The past is past. Let bygones be bygones. Forgive and forget. O God, if only it were that simple. Cheated, violated once, we want to avoid being cheated again by handing out premature forgiveness. But in the long run, moving too quickly will cheat us of the peace you promise from true forgiveness. Teach us the difference.

Remind us that true forgiveness comes *after* acknowledging deed and doer. Strengthen us when we opt to avoid this pain.

Show us, instead, that premature forgiveness comes from a slothful kind of faith, not the kind practiced by your Son. He shook sinners out of trees so they could mend their ways. He willed stones to drop from hypocrites' hands so they could repent of their double standard. He called a demon a demon, so "Mob" could know what was done to them and become a single, whole, healed self. He recognized sinners by name so they could be urged to go and sin no more. No premature forgiveness here, no generic exemption.

Reassure us that we need not literally face doer or deed; forgiveness can happen in the room of the soul. Give us pen and paper, tape recorder, or computer to compose poems, songs, letters, prayers. Send us to paint, sculpt, whittle, . . . anything to bring us face to face with pain and the ones who caused it, and to tell of its weight in our lives. Stand with us to call a spade a spade, claim our wounds, and say good-bye. We are ready to be done with this, despite pity and grief.

Then, only then, will we know the difference between premature and true forgiveness. Celebrate with us that, yes, bygones can *then* be bygones.

Words of Light

Live as children of light. . . . Everything exposed by the light becomes visible. (Ephesians 5:8,13, NIV)

Compassion Fatigue

So much need, O God, in the face of violence, so little time and energy to do anything about it. An overload of statistics, plights, pleas numbs us; we are sick of being afraid that we will be a statistic-victim, and we are sick of hearing endlessly about those who are.

We need a break from trying to offset need by deed.

Some of us do compassionate deeds as mate, friend, kin, in the name of love, which makes the need no less wearing. Some of us do it for a living, which makes the pain no easier to bear; some, as volunteers, which makes the pleas no easier to leave behind; some, just in our daily lives. All of us are tired. Tireless Guardian, we ashamedly confess we can't do one more thing or hear one more sad tale.

We are tempted to give up until we think of the wondrous goose. In your wisdom, you provided geese a V in which to fly, a main goose in point position to break through the wind for following comrades. Watch them swap positions. Hear them honk encouragement. No goose, wise Creator, is meant to fly forever in point position. Geese take turns, take up slack, in the natural rhythm of things. Surely we are as wise as they.

Go with us as we ask for help and take breaks from leading the V. Reassure us that it is okay to be sick and tired, that compassion fatigue is a temporary malady, that our lament will be brief. Inspire others to pick up the slack and support those called to fly point positions.

By naming our needs and asking for help, we feel an updraft of fresh air where we can rest a while, knowing you are wind beneath our wings.

Words of Light

He gives power to the tired and worn out, and strength to the weak. (Isaiah 40:29, TLB)

No Negotiation

When battle lines are drawn in the sands of our lives, if we know we are right, why negotiate? If we don't, we win. No need for further discussion. Whose fault is it, Prince of Peace, that there is so little evidence of peace-seeking? Who fumbled the art of negotiation?

They did. That's easy—for we feel besieged and threatened; enemies surround us. The trouble is, these days enemies can be defined simply as anyone who disagrees with us. As stakes get higher, the fiercer the violence we wage and the more determined we are to hold out, rather than to meet on common ground in families, neighborhoods, governments, countries, and churches. Dialogue is for losers, peace for wimps.

"Aha!" we shout gleefully when yet another enemy rides over the horizon of our daily lives. We take aim and, *kaboom*, blow them away. Favorite weapons in our arsenal for waging daily, nonnegotiable violence are gossip; silence and rejection; verses, slogans, and bumper stickers; piety and positions of power; bombs, bullets, fists, and shouts. We are a crowd of mouths, Lord, with not a listening ear or an outstretched hand in sight.

Stand between your squabbling children, and hold each one in a hand. Unstop our ears so we can hear common concerns, similar desires, and prayers for safety, well-being. Form our fist-making hands into a circle of compromise where we can't tell whose fingers are whose because we are clinging so tightly to resolve for mutual peace.

Be the hand that holds us together.

Words of Light

If you keep on biting and devouring each another, watch out or you will be destroyed by each other. (Galatians 5:15, NIV)

Anxiety Attacked

Hearts pound, mouths dry like spit on stone, ears ring in deafening alarm: Anxiety is tethering us to the violence done to us. Victims once, Lord, we fear being victims forever unless we get a grip, get control, get over it.

Yet we cry to you from this pit of anxiety. How can we not be anxious when we've been through the valley of the shadow of death at the hand of those who would destroy us? How can we not be anxious when we've looked into the face of evil? For some of us, that face was stranger; for others, it was parent, mate, friend. How can we not be anxious about whom we can trust? How can we not be anxious when we know too well how quickly predators attack, ambushing us in our innocence?

We dare not move from this hunkered-down place of immobility, for some of us were threatened even greater harm if we did; some of us assume we do not deserve to; some of us simply accept this anxious stuckness as inevitable.

Place your steadying hands on our pounding hearts and sweating faces. Guide us to those who can accompany us back into the lives we've been too anxious to resume. Lift up our eyes to possibilities of bold recovery.

Strengthen us for confronting our molesters, rapists, muggers, the disbelievers. To remain paralyzed in anxiety is to give them double victory, for they will have taken our spirits, as well as our belongings, our bodies. But violators cannot take these things without our surrender, so be with us as we dig in, brace for recovery. We want to go on, and we will, despite anxious moments briefly encountered as we pass through and beyond the valleys.

Words of Light

I say to you, do not be anxious for your life. (Matthew 6:25, NASB)

Moving On

It's hard to believe, but time has passed since those awful violent days, just as people said it would. Time passes, time heals, they promised. Some of us were grown up when violence struck and pain began. Some of us were little kids, dear God, remember?

Either way, they were right: time has passed. But it hasn't healed, and we are stranded like boats on a sandbar: We can't go forward or backward.

Help us to wriggle off this barren stretch of life where time has stopped. To remain stranded here is still to be victim, not victor.

Choosing a direction towards victory is confusing, for we want to move ahead even as we yearn to turn the clock back . . .

. . . to gentler dailyness before violence contaminated our lives;

. . . before memory of violence insisted that we must grieve in order to be healed;

. . . before we faced choices about forgiving, so we can be free;

. . . before we wanted to learn revenge, which is rarely as satisfying as supposed;

. . . before we had to accept that justice might not happen;

. . . before we understood that the effort to recover must be ours because no one can do it for us.

You can understand, then, Creator of all time and tides, that it is easier to stay on our sandbars of pain than it is to slide into unknown currents. Nudge us gently into possibilities, for they lead to renewal. Remind us that it is high time we move toward your voice calling to us over the waves.

Words of Light

Save me, O God, For the waters have come up to my soul.

I have sunk in deep mire . . . I have come into deep waters, and a flood overflows me. I am weary with my crying. . . . (Psalm 69:1-3, NASB)

Lay aside the old self. . . . Put on the new self. (Ephesians 4:22-24, NASB)

We Are Them: A Confession

O God, not only is our world violent, *we* are violent. We bait the trap of evil ourselves when we make wrong choices. No wonder you keep reminding us to choose life; you know our tendencies! Sometimes acting alone and sometimes acting together, we hurt others. Hear our confession for mild and brutal deeds, for passive and aggressive acts of . . .

   . . . cynicism and apathy, quiet forms of violence;

   . . . lukewarm concern when we could care as passionately as you do;

   . . . violent thoughts (if thoughts are deeds, then we've maimed many);

   . . . not speaking up when we hear crude, bigoted, or inflammatory remarks, jokes;

   . . . willfully misunderstanding others' points of view;

   . . . holding grudges and withholding true forgiveness;

   . . . lashing out in spite and sarcasm;

   . . . making gestures, rude faces to intimidate others, especially kids;

   . . . yelling, hitting, slapping, and trying to justifying ourselves (we have no excuse);

   . . . ignoring signs of family or child abuse and not getting involved;

   . . . not being Good Samaritans for fear of getting hurt ourselves, and so letting someone suffer, even die, doubly betrayed, as we passed by.

We fall so far short of who we can be. We fail in small ways, even if not in big ways. Forgive us, God of mercy, when our deeds do not match our words about peace and love. Help us to bring word and deed together like hands in prayer, two halves of a whole, forgiven and renewed person. Amen.

Words of Light

Look to yourself. . . . For if any one thinks he is something, when he is nothing, he deceives himself. . . . Each man will have to bear his own load. (Galatians 6:1,3,5, RSV)

Violence Tempered

How Does Your Garden Grow?

Once we've stared evil in the face, O God, we don't see things the same way we did before. Events look like we are seeing them through a dirty fish bowl, and faith, like beauty and joy, grows shriveled from disuse. We live *as if* you and we had died.

Since, we reason, violence is waiting in ambush, why plant a garden, rake leaves, or make angels in the snow? What's the point in watching diets, taking healthful walks, or saving pennies? It seems senseless, Lord, to tend lives when, *rat-a-tat,* they can be ruined in the pull of a trigger, toss of a bomb, bump of a carjacker, footstep of an intruder, cadence of a warrior boot.

We are giving up without a protest, *as if* evil had already had the last word. Even as we respect evil's crude power, we yearn to say "Enough!" and retrieve what it stole: the power to live *as if* hope is alive, healing, possible.

As you did with loaves and fishes long ago, multiply our hope and energy into more. Thus nourished, we will live *as if* the light cannot be put out; *as if* your will is for good, not bad; *as if* we have a sporting chance to turn this thing around.

Life in a dingy fishbowl is distorted, Lord. The view is no good, and the stench from stagnating hope is overpowering. Sweeten the waters where we tread. Clean the lens through which we look . . . even at evil . . . with eyes of *as-if* faith.

Words of Light

If God is for us, who is against us? (Romans 8:31, RSV)

Faith is the assurance of things hoped for, the conviction of things not seen. (Hebrews 11:1, RSV)

Credo of Light in Darkness

I need to believe beyond the present darkness, for it threatens to stop me in my tracks. Steady me, God of infinite resources, as I collect my beliefs like candles to light the way as I move through this dark tunnel of doubt and uncertainty. In that hope, I believe . . .

. . . in a God who cries first when we are violated, terrorized;

. . . that there are pathfinders to follow from the horror of violence;

. . . in a God who never wills that violence be done to me or others;

. . . that there is something to redeem from our pain and fury;

. . . in a God who, however, does not send pain for that or any purpose;

. . . that there are good people who will restore my faith in goodness;

. . . that I am a child of a loving Parent who knows my name;

. . . that there is a bright, vigorous, and useful future for me;

. . . in a God who equips me with skills and strengths to reach that future.

I also believe . . .

  . . .

  . . .

  . . .

. . . that there is room for doubt in the midst of belief because I believe in a God who accepts my unbelief when it is the only prayer I have to offer.

Inspire me to add new truths as they reveal themselves in my life, as I proceed through this present darkness. Along the way, Lord, help my unbelief.

Words of Light

"I do believe. Help me in my unbelief!" (Mark 9:24, NASB)

Parentheses of Faith

On one hand, good and gracious God, we find you and all you represent: creation, beauty, seasons; love and lovers; children and kittens; rainbow hope; everlasting rest and everyday companionship—all the things of which you said, ". . . and it was good."

On the other hand, we find incredible darkness: betrayal, injustice, suffering, apathy, crime, bigotry, persecution.

We stand in the middle, torn like the turkey wishbone: Shall we be hopeful or fearful people? Many of us know firsthand why it makes the most sense to be fearful. We read statistics and find our names written there. All of us know violence secondhand: Friends, loved ones, strangers across the world connect us to pain and sorrow. Their cries stick in our throats.

Fear versus hope: How can we live within such parentheses?

We sometimes envy those whose faith fits on a bumper sticker or sweatshirt, for they seem to avoid wrestling with the question, "Why does bad happen?" It just does, though, it just does, and our dialogues with you fill reams, not inches, of prayer and thought. Bless our conversations.

Remind us that in a world of free will, we can't have good without bad, a head without a tail. Good and evil exist side by side, even as we yearn for them not to. Reassure us that you are present with us in both as we choose, respond, and react. Strengthen us to live the question and to not settle for superficial answers that will leave us uneasy and still alone in the dark.

Fear versus hope: Our choice is the hinge upon which your will for us can become evident. Therefore, Lord of all seasons, we choose hope. It offers us energy for life within parentheses of dark and light.

Words of Light

"I am the A and the Z—the Beginning and the End."
(Revelation 21:6, TLB)

Hard Choice

Targets. What, O God, would meanness be without them? So easily we become targets by being a certain race, gender, age, appearance, . . . by simply being in the wrong place at the wrong time. Whether targeted by random violence or personalized brutality, we get snagged on what to do next, like a fox that comes upon a wall of brambles scant seconds ahead of larger, snarling jaws. What now? We pace here, Lord, like the fox, deciding: "Go around, go over, go under, go through? Fight back? Surrender?"

We claim the only piece of this violence—random or personalized—that we can control: our response to it. Yet, O God, this, too, is a burden. We are caught between actions reflecting hope or despair. Which one to choose? How to act? Hard choice.

Restore our perspective, Lord, for we are focused only on calamity. Looking ahead, we fear that the slobbering jaws will strike again, if only in memory. Lift us to your shoulders, so we can see beyond the brambly wall. The view and its promise give tired spirits a boost. Remind us that we are not helpless once we untangle ourselves from brambles and scramble over, under, around, or through the wall. We can talk, share feelings, grieve through tears, writing, painting, journaling. We have you, like a fox has a den, for recovery.

With that promise, urge us to lick our wounds, to take care of ourselves as we would after surgery. Our bodies suffer indigestion, insomnia, aches as we grieve. Keep us sensible lest we target ourselves. We can't make pain go away by overeating or boozing, so help us to find better comforters.

We are grateful for your assurance that helplessness and anxiety are not places we will stay stuck—after all, you helped us get beyond that wall! You promise comfort to those who dare to mourn. Lord of life-and-death choices, remind us that we claimed your promise when we made our choices and figured out how to elude pursuers.

Finding comfort is a journey that begins with the moment of shock, discovering we are the target for someone else's spite. But then there is always hope, even if it is only hope to get through this next hour. Guide us to companionship through books, media, people who've "been there, done that" and lived to frolic and dance again on the far sides of brambled walls.

Hear our prayers and wails in the darkness of the memory of pursuit and attack. Help us also to remember and to celebrate what we did to escape, survive, overcome. Having done that, with your help, O God, we will find sufficient strength to live with the questions: Why evil? Why us?

For now, though, it is enough to know that you will be with us, not only in the questions but as life goes where we wash the car, get groceries, feed the cat, plant a tree, bounce a ball, hum a tune. Like a fox sunning itself on top of the wall, we can look back at being a target, down at the brambles of indecision about how to respond, and ahead to unthought-of possibilities for joy.

Words of Light

You have been my help; don't leave me, don't abandon me. . . . Have faith, do not despair. (Psalm 27:9,14, GNB)

Splatters

Violence splatters like water from a mud puddle when a car hurries through, soiling us all. We shiver through the news, shake our heads over newspapers and magazines. These, O God, are caustic times.

Rather than making us more fearful, let this splattering of awareness be an invitation to reclaim streets and neighborhoods, attitude and vision. Violence can only thrive in a vacuum, as water can only collect like a mud puddle in a hole. We stand at water's edge and wonder how to fill the hole up.

In our uneasiness, guide us to find creative ways to respond to communal and personal violence; we feel overwhelmed. Help us to stand with your special servant Elie Wiesel and echo his words from a speech: "I believe in small miracles. . . . Help one person here, reach out there. They may not seem small to those who receive them." You, O God, honor our smallest efforts toward peacemaking, even if all we do is change our attitudes. Inspire us by others who, after tragedy, can mount national campaigns, establish foundations and funds, write books, and launch movements. They met a problem head-on with action, not reactions. They lead us.

Nudge us so that instead of wringing our hands, we use them to build Habitat for Humanity homes, to serve soup, to push playground swings, to hold lonely ones, to turn book pages as we minister to those who turn to violence as a last resort, out of frustration and despair. Use us to do small miracles.

If we still fret, O God, remind us that we can best find hope to change the tenor of these days by doing. Teach us that hope is not a visitor who seeks us, and that we must open our double-bolted doors to go find it. Be with us as we venture beyond our fears and doubt and follow your Son into the world.

Words of Light

Let us pursue the things which make for peace and the building up of one another. (Romans 14:19, NASB)

Blueprint for Recovery

A stranger lives in my skin. Familiar landmarks are unrecognizable when seen through eyes that once looked evil in the face. I am grateful to have survived, O God, but I have no idea who I am, what to do, where to go.

Violence does that, Lord. With its vile acts, it rips through ordinary lives like a tornado through town. It picks us up and sets us down a lifetime away from goodness, pleasure, relaxation, fun, hope, energy. We feel lost even from ourselves once we assess the devastation: Trust and security are gone; assumptions are crumbled; optimism is buried beneath reality. Very little is recognizable in this new landscape of victim. Not much seems sturdy enough to stand on.

How can we rebuild? How can we ever hope to have a place where battered bodies and spirits can live secure, hopeful, proud again? Having fun, taking a vacation, telling a joke, and sleeping in the sun seem as impossible as sprouting wings. What is left in the rubble of naivete and trust, yes, even in you, God, that can be used to start over?

We beg from our knees: *Help us to rebuild.* Give us a blueprint for recovery, a road map to healing. We are buried beneath the debris of others' dumping. Hear us calling you from the filth. Find us. Help us to dig out. Be the foundation upon which we rebuild.

Words of Light

Thou dost show me the path of life. (Psalm 16:11 RSV)

"With God all things are possible." (Matthew 19:26, NASB)

Riding Out the Grief

Violation, O God, is ice in the mind. Hold us in the warmth of your embrace as we tremble in bone-chilling disbelief of what happened. Fear has become reality since violence struck a blow. What now? Our world is different, our beliefs overturned. It is too much to bear.

Be with us in the aftermath of undeserved and frightening victimizations, personal or communal, random or deliberate, old or new. We are caught on the barb of someone else's meanness and contaminated by their violence. We are frozen in shock.

Give us courage to wail like the lost children we are. Open the floodgates of tears so they can sluice the toxins from our bodies. Assure us, O God, that we will not drown in this river of tears, for there are sun-warmed boulders to rest upon. We can climb onto them, as if into your lap, whenever we tire during the journey of recovery. Remind us that buffeting waves of emotion, like currents in river rapids, are okay. We don't have to be rational, nice, or calm about this; reassure us that we won't get stuck in our tears. Praise without lament is not honest; accept our grief as evidence of our trust in you.

Our grief, God of current and tides, is taking us somewhere new. We must simply believe it is, hold on, and keep moving.

Words of Light

In hope against hope he believed. . . . He did not waver in unbelief, but grew strong in faith, . . . (Romans 4:18,20, NASB)

Broody Hen

We gather here, encircling God, beneath your broody wings to rest. We are tired from thinking about what happened and exhausted from the fear and memory. We've talked all we can right now. We've been brave, steadfast, and valiant when seeking justice and healing. We've persevered in our quest to find you in this awful thing, and we have found you. But, we cry, our hearts are so heavy, our minds empty.

Find and hold us. We can't be strong and big right now. Hold us, loving Gatherer, like the lost children we are. Lullaby and soothe us so we may feel your love, as children find security with a favorite blanket, a thumb in the mouth, a toy or special teddy bear.

Even though we are grown up and strong, we need you to stay extra close in the dark nights when

. . . *we wake in nightmares, replaying nasty deeds.* Make them into safe pictures in a book that tells a freeing tale that we put away and look at when we wish.

. . . *we hesitate to be happy, sometimes feeling soiled and distressed from others' acts.* Remind us that our strength is your joy and that you came to bring us abundant life.

. . . *we are tempted to give up and give in to self-destruction, accomplishing what others tried to do.* Remind us of third-day risings despite others' evil intentions. We know you want no less for us.

. . . *we feel childish and unsure.* Scoot us beneath your broody wings like a hen her chicks, and remind us that grief is good; that tears are a wondrous cleansing gift; and that you are making all things new, even this awful thing that was never your idea.

. . . *we falter at moments like these, tired, discouraged.* Assure us that progress is not a straight, flat line: A heart monitor that reads like that is not about life but about death! Help us to roll with the ups and downs, celebrating the variety of feelings we experience.

We can rest now, knowing that you are as close as a prayerful thought, a sigh in our sleep. You are our refuge, our sanctuary. Thank you for thumbs and blankets, familiar verses, songs, rituals—whatever brings us comfort. They are gifts from your hands that spread like wings over us while we sleep, your warm presence most comforting of all.

Words of Light

"How often I have longed to gather your children together, as a hen gathers her chicks under her wings . . . ." (Matthew 23:37, NIV)

Clip and Save

Where is the *hope?* we wail. Where is any *good* in these abrasive times? Oh, dear God, we are so discouraged and downhearted; send us signs of hope and reassurance.

While we're waiting, life would be easier if you would fix everything for us, flush the bad, restore the good. In one fell swoop, God of Noah and doves, you could tidy up the mess we've made. It looks hopeless.

Forgive us for wanting, again, easy ways out and for missing the signs of your ongoing presence. Renew our spirits and open our eyes: Your doves are all around us in the lives of people who reach out, care, and do good despite reasons to give up and despair. The folks who helped in Oklahoma and at other sites of tragedy have counterparts in all corners of the globe. God of Light, how could we have missed this? It's easy; we've been looking down into the rubble, not up into the eyes of people who hear your call.

To start us looking in a new direction, we will clip and save four news stories about hope-full folks. Bless them and their deeds.

-
-
-
-

Balancing concern with trust, we will continue to note hope-full news makers. Inspired by their lives, we pledge to *be* one of them, your doves to a world not yet drowning in its misery. No, Lord, we can't speak of war without peace, despair without hope, the cowardice of terrorists and bullies without the beauty of heroes (the extraordinary ones and the daily ones who only set out to do one small thing, to make their contribution).

And before you know it, Lord of loaves and fishes, that one small thing has blossomed into something that makes a difference, even if for only one person, one situation. The tide will be turning.

Words of Light

Everyone helps his neighbor, and says . . . , "Take courage!" (Isaiah 41:6, RSV)

A Child by any Other Name

"I must deserve bad things," we conclude after violence strikes. "I must be unlovable," we decide, deducing our value from how the way others treat us. Hear our self-doubt, O God, for violent attitudes and behaviors contaminate us, clobber our self-esteem.

Then, sad to say, it becomes tempting for us to agree with the haters, bigots, molesters, rapists, terrorists and bullies, the manipulators and schemers, the thieves, car-jackers, and stalkers, the ones who leave us to conclude that we don't deserve any better than to be bait for their traps, carrion for their hungers. Do we?

Violation begets shame. Hear our self-doubt, O God.

"I have called you by name, you are mine," a Voice says, interrupting our worries. "Called you by name," we repeat the wonderful assurance.

You call us by name, number the hairs of our heads, guard our comings in and goings out, lift us to high places and set your angels over us. How then can we doubt our value with such overwhelming evidence to the contrary! We reclaim our honor. With your validation in our ears, we can protest the devaluing we've endured. Bullies are wrong, and we do deserve good things!

In self-doubting times, guide us to know you as a loving parent who wills wholeness for each of your children, whom you know and tend personally. We are grateful that you are a name-calling God.

Words of Light

I have called you by name, you are mine. (Isaiah 43:1, RSV)

A Tentative First Step

God of mercy, what is forgiving? Where are the lines between it and denying, colluding, excusing, exempting? Can we forgive and demand justice? And what of the enormity of the grievance and pain; it has an integrity that must not be denied. It may be possible to forgive but not to live as if the violation never happened. Of all the unfairness about violence, O God, forgiveness seems the most unfair. Victims lose twice: They endure violation and then have to give up anger in order to forgive. *We are not ready to do more than consider forgiveness as an option.*

Ease our confusion and help us to understand that forgiveness is not exemption, that we can pray for those who hurt us without being their "buddy." Reeducate us, Lord, to the truth that expressing righteous anger is not the same as "getting even." Keep us from joining the cycle of violence.

Forgiving, on second thought, may be the best option for treating ourselves fairly. After all, what is fair about staying stuck to a past event like gum on the underside of a table? Isn't it fairer to ourselves to find a way to get unstuck? Forgiving, in your hands, Lord, is one of those strong currents that can move us through life's confusing rapids.

Nudge us when we prefer to stay stuck rather than to relinquish our powerful bitterness. Move us on, Lord, when we are addicted to the memory of old pain, stuck in the miserable fairness of not forgiving. When we forgive, we set someone free. We release the captives, who were us.

In time, Lord, in time, perhaps we will give forgiveness a try.

Words of Light

[Peter asked,] "How often should I forgive a brother who sins against me? Seven times?" "No!" Jesus replied, "seventy times seven!" (Matthew 18:21,22, TLB)

Meeting Hope

Hope has a face and healing hands, O God. They belong to those who surround us in dark hours of remembering and terror. They buffer us against the faces and hands we feared would continue to wield power in our lives. We retreat from the threat, and then we crouch, vulnerable, hopeless, like a pile of old clothes in a dark closet. Finally violators lose the weight of power and violence when other hands and faces spot us, pick us up, and lead us into the light of a good day, a renewed life, fresh hope. Despair, in the presence of our rescuers, is merely out-of-season clothing.

O God of doves and rainbows, we know then what hope looks like when family, advocates, friends, even strangers stop to help. They bring us hope, those who have shared similar fates, and who accompany us through the dark tunnel of crisis, the recurring memories, the system that sometimes bruises us even more.

Thanks to them, we are empowered for the hard work of recovery. Thanks to them, we know you as a personal and present resource. We pause in our journey of healing and turn from the awfulness that brought us to this moment to name your delegates of hope in our lives:

-

-

Behind these faces, O God, we recognize yours; beneath supporting hands of friends and helpers, we feel your strong grasp. Thank you. Help us in time to be channels for others of this hand-and-face hope.

Words of Light

This is how we know what love is. (1 John 3:16, GNB)

The Prize Goes to the Winner

It doesn't much matter, Source of Life, where and when and to what degree violence tagged us with its sticky hands. Its leftovers are pretty much the same. "You're it!" it screams in glee, watching as we, like pricked balloons, fall deflated in a heap. Life is gloom and doom, we begin to think, and then we add "Amen," as if that were all it is.

"Amen" to violation? Not hardly. Give up good things? No way.

For what, God of belly laughs and rib-tickling fun, are we to do with the rest of your wonderful world? Once tagged by violence, must we be forever grim, underachieving, losers? Must we give up love, pleasure, laughing, play? Not hardly. Inspire us to claim these gifts again, lest the bullies win at tag. Bless our smiles and drives to excel, move on, enjoy, even help.

We replay your reminder to become like children. No matter how ravaged by violation we may be, renew in us, O God, a childlike sense of awe at grass growing in a sidewalk crack, the smell of plain earth, the taste of raindrops, the melody of a bumblebee's song. They remind us how to be joyful simply for being alive. Bless us with reminders of our own dreams, aspirations, plans, and goals. Violation is just a detour; guide us past it.

We yearn to believe life can be good for us, even with its underbelly. We search for verses that say you want us to enjoy vacations, bonuses, family, birthday parties, peace, and business success. We listen even in dreams with one ear cocked to hear you say, "Be happy and free, my child. It's okay to smile and play and enjoy what you have." We keep our eyes peeled for signs of your blessing on our smiles.

But as we do, we still worry and ask again, "How can we face personal violation, decaying cities, mean streets, secret-laden families, and dividing churches, and then dare to play golf on velvet greens, to doze on beaches and mountaintops, to putter in field and stream?"

"How can you not?" we hear you ask. Would the world be any less bleak if we added our long faces to it? Would creation be less endangered if we avoided beach, mountain, desert, forest? Does being successful, happy, healed mean we can't also help? Would even one toxic family be saved if we refused to enjoy our own?

Nope.

Turn us on our heels, Lord, to face violence and boldly to say, "Not it! You cannot keep me captive from my world." Like children getting ready for recess, we accept your gift of renewal, of miraculous small healings, as we take back our lives.

In that strength and promise, O God, we now can do something about our troubled world. It takes energy to fix broken-down things; it takes creative, childlike savvy to come up with new ideas. Where better to find vision and energy for healing and re-creation than in enjoying your gifts? They are the hard-won prize, not the penalty, for being victors.

Words of Light

"Unless you . . . become like children, you will never enter the kingdom . . . ." (Matthew 18:3, RSV)

He restores my soul. . . . (Psalm 23:3, NASB)

We confidently and joyfully look forward to actually becoming all that God has had in mind for us to be. (Romans 5:2, TLB)

Violence Redeemed

Prescription Filled

We confess, great Physician, that when we are confronted with a problem, we feel a nervous desire to act. "Do something!" we shout. We find it especially difficult these days to be passive in the face of hate and violence, deadly maladies that contaminate our lives.

Restrain us from overreaction. As with other maladies, the cure might be worse than the disease: Is backlash any less violent than its provocation? Is a counterpunch less damaging than a first swing?

Help us to discover long-lasting, nonviolent antidotes, for they are far more potent than the *anti*violence that shows up in such guises as the armed assassins at an anti-abortion clinic, too. To be nonviolent is to focus on what we can do: learn tolerance, teach parenting and relating skills, practice manners and courtesy, strengthen justice systems.

Above all, creator God, we can prescribe respect for diversity. So many of our attacks on one another are over differences of color, creed, status, choices, lifestyle, opinion, even over how we perceive, experience, and describe you. Did you hear about the person who shot a spouse over an interpretation of your Word? Sad but true.

Surely you who created us wonderfully different from one another, down to the prints of our fingers, never intended us to kill over those differences! Cure us of a warring madness that is making us sick, so sick, Lord of sojourners, that we are unsafe drivers, a sobering new symptom. As we ponder symptoms and causes, remind us that, as the nonviolent, we can learn skillful, healing conflict resolution. *Give us a reconciling attitude when it would be easier to retaliate or escalate.* We can learn to identify triggers of violence. *Help us to be willing to be the first to disarm. Bring us face to face with those we hate.*

Reread us stories of your Son who won by word, not by sword. *Remind us what true victory is.* Open our eyes to see the connection between fanning flames of hate with rhetoric and the action it brings. *We confess we're not blameless if we keep silent, echo, or applaud.*

Remind us that prevention is still the best antidote. *Give us, God of generations, energy to be role models of non-violence.* Equip us with the most life-sustaining antidote of all: courage to live as if peace is possible and hope is a viable choice.

Words of Light

I pray that you may enjoy good health and that all may go well with you, even as your soul is getting along well. (3 John 2, NIV)

In all things we are more than conquerors through him who loved us. (Romans 8:37, RSV)

Pathfinders

In this dark, mean-minded world of ours, God, we are wandering around like kids lost in a cave. Touched by violence, personal or random, we inch perilously close to the edge of despair, unable to see where we are going. We butt our heads against stone walls of revenge. We crouch in fear, rather than risk falling while searching for an exit. Send us guides who've traveled dark passages before; send us pathfinders.

God of action, remind us that guides don't find us; we must find them. Let us remember and be guided by those who went down, through, and beyond the deepest darkness imaginable: wars, the Holocaust, torture, family violence, random wickedness. No matter how deep the cave where they were plunged, there are those who triumphed to live and laugh and love again, respecting darkness for what it is but not remaining its captive:

• Maya Angelou, survivor of abuse, poet, author

• Elie Wiesel, Holocaust survivor, Nobel Peace Prize winner

•

•

•

•

• _____ *(your name)*

In time we will add our names to this list, so someone else may follow a path out of the dark.

Words of Light

In all these things we are more than conquerors through him who loved us. (Romans 8:37, RSV)

Every one helps his neighbor, and says . . . , "Take courage!" (Isaiah 41:6, RSV)

Dot to Dot

Just as the dentist numbs our nerves to keeps us from screaming with pain, so our feelings are numbed to protect us until it is time, sooner or later, to look at what's what, to make plans for the rest of our lives, and to move on through the darkness. *O God, can we do it?*

Help us to endure thawing, even if at first it prickles like a hand that's been asleep. We're coming back to life in the wake of violation, arriving in a brand new world. We are grateful to have been spared; give us courage to live as if that were true!

When we get impatient, remind us that mending from ordeals is not like riding a train that runs on a certain schedule. Rather, through your grace, healing is a promised destination on a journey that takes as long as necessary to complete.

Bless our memories, sharpen our wits, and loosen our tongues for telling our tales. Inspire our visions for tomorrow. Send us worthy listeners and advocates to be companions on a path that feels like drawing a dot-to-dot picture: We come upon a discovery here, a new feeling and understanding there, a fresh thought somewhere else, recurring or brand new joys.

Dot-to-dot, here we go, not allowing others' vile intentions to hold us back. When the picture is completed, we will have connected the most amazing self-portrait of a mended child, created, as always, O God, in your image and intention. Steady our hands as we connect parts of a picture that darkness and evil cannot ever erase.

Words of Light

We spend our years as a tale that is told. (Psalm 90:9, KJV)
Thou dost show me the path of life; . . . . (Psalm 16:11 RSV)

Excavations

Memories, God of history, are hardly as sweet as poets and songwriters claim. Hardly as sweet, yet more important, for they are crucial to our healing, healing to the reality of what brought us to this painful moment: Violence struck us.

Whether the deed was large or small, whether we were child or adult, betrayal happens in a split second and then is not measured in size or age but in effect. For some of us, betrayal was so recent that we still have bruises; for some, it was long ago. Home, war, mall, backyard, it hardly matters where or when. We just want to be freed of this pain that rightfully belongs to bullies, misusers, enemies. Help us to send it back.

In that hope, we ask you for courage to believe ourselves and for wits to find validation, even proof, if possible, for our memories. If not, then we ask for bravery to claim them as the truth we know them to be. Give us stamina to withstand advice to "forgive and forget" until it is time to do that. Give us resolve to ignore well-meaning folks who advise that we forgive, as well as those who because of their role prefer that we forget.

Stand with us as we try not to forget, as we recall your promise about the truth setting us free. Hold us as we seek truth, struggling to find out, "Are we accurate? Are we distorting, imagining?" Lead us to answers and acceptance; open doors to your promised redemption and healing. We know that in your hands, our recovered memories are buried treasures of hope and new life. Bless our digging.

Words of Light

"I will give you the treasures of darkness . . . In order that you may know that it is I, the LORD, . . . who calls you by your name." (Isaiah 45:3, NASB)

Truth and Consequences

We are taught from earliest Sunday school days to turn the other cheek, to judge not, to check the logs in our own eyes, to forgive and forget.

Yet, God, to do so after violence can be as deceitful as the bad deeds themselves. Reassure us that we can faithfully forgive while we require justice and consequences, because demanding justice is different from launching retaliation.

Consequences are the natural order: b follows a, just as resetting boundaries follows violence, especially in families. We cannot be okay and continue to be the people our families require. Moving on is a consequence we can painfully choose.

As we do, steady us when our violators act outraged. Help us to bear the fact that molesting parents act brokenhearted when children leave and don't return for holidays. That raping spouses act incredulous when violated mates freeze up, turn away, move out. That batterers act shocked when bruised and broken targets flee fists, words, weapons. That sadistic parents act betrayed when scarred children turn on them, giving what they've gotten. What goes around comes around.

It is baffling to bear violators compounding violence by accusing us of hurting them! We feel crazy, mean, and disloyal. Be with us when the lure of collusion tempts us. Keep us firm in claiming our truth; you lived it with us. Stay with us now, too, as we learn that allowing consequences is a part of forgiveness. Help us to learn to let them happen; we long to be free.

Bolster earlier supporters who now question our firm resolve and stiff hearts. Reassure them that we are simply letting nature take its course: Violence begets consequences. O God, ease the loneliness, our consequence.

Thank you for courage to face violence and disconnect from those who inflict it. Leaving them to their consequences is the least we can do.

Words of Light

For the wrongdoer will be paid back for the wrong he has done, and there is no partiality. (Colossians 3:25, RSV)

Smorgasbord

A homesick day today, O God. Been thinking about the aroma of tasseling corn; amazing. Thought I'd buried that in a deep, deep hole: The place where corn grew was nasty, evil.

What is wrong with us when we are homesick for those places that hold memories of trauma, unpleasantness, or even terror? Can places and other circumstances of our violations be okay? Like oil and water, happy and sad, good and evil, they can't mix with the here and now. Right?

Help us, God who created oil and water. Let two realities be true at the same time. To recover from assault on bodies and senses, whether random or very, very personal, we must let good and bad—both/and—exist in that time and place. We can claim what was good and leave what was bad, toxic, harmful.

Be with us if we feel disloyal to the wounded self when we get nostalgic for sights, smells, sounds from abusive childhoods or once-upon-fun sites of recent muggings, assaults. Violations don't take place in hell. The places where they occur become hell later, if we let them.

Should robbery victims avoid all motels because they were robbed in one? Tempting, Lord. Should children grown to adult squelch all memory of swings and sandboxes and people who were good because of those who were evil? Seems safest, sanest. Do all ocean sprays, fields of tasseling corn, Christmas trees, bowls of popcorn need to smell less wonderful in our memories because of a separate dirty deed? Do we have to discard all bedrooms, malls, parking lots, street corners, jogging paths, foreign shores, and holidays? Our lists can go on and on, O God, but the bottom-line question remains the same: Must we hate all the old before we can love and live in the new world we are constructing for ourselves on this side of violence? As we live that question in our sometimes confusing daily lives, remind us that "nothing is unclear in itself" (Romans 14:14 NASB). Help us to approach these memories as if we were checking out a smorgasbord buffet: Be with us as we take what is good for us and leave behind what isn't.

Words of Light

Fix your thoughts on what is true and good and right. Think about things that are pure and lovely. (Philippians 4:8, TLB)

Just a Hunch

What wonderful resources you give us, Creator God, so we can enjoy your world: our senses of taste and smell; our emotions; traits like curiosity; intuitions that lead to life-saving, split-second decisions when we are walking through shadowy valleys in the presence of well-organized enemies.

We get a hunch, a flash of intuition, and it proves right: We don't get on a certain elevator, take a particular sidewalk, don't become involved with particular people or enlist in certain causes. "Danger, danger" we feel flashing through our senses. We recognize you in this primitive, sensory awareness that can keep us from danger. Help us to hone skills of self-preservation, for they are a gift from you.

We are, as the psalmist says, "wondrously made." Accepting that gift, we are grateful that you endowed us with intuition, hunches, "funny feelings." They can save our lives as effectively as if we were still avoiding beasts in long-gone jungles. Resources of vigilance and assessment, not paranoia that binds us in fear, are tickets to freedom in your promised abundant life.

Words of Light

Thank you for making me so wonderfully complex! It is amazing to think about. Your workmanship is marvelous—and how well I know it. (Psalm 139:14, TLB)

The mature . . . because of practice have their senses trained to discern good and evil. (Hebrews 5:14, NASB)

Good Old Days

It's hard to tell what decade this is, O God, for our homes and offices overflow with memorabilia, collectibles, antiques, and just plain leftovers. Today looks like yesterday. Decorators call it "retrospective." We know it for what it is: homesickness.

We long for the good old days when folks were optimistic and proud, you know, the pre-violence days. Back when the most popular exhibit at the 1939 World's Fair was "Voice of the Future." We dreamed great dreams in those days: superhighways, peacetime gadgets, cars, houses, and jobs for all. Inspired, we built cities, schools and neighborhoods that worked and streets that were safe . . . for a while.

Lord, Lord, what went wrong? Something did, that's for sure. Now, instead of learning from past mistakes that brought wars and a mean-spirited mood instead of peace, we keep trying to go back. More than nostalgic, we're lost. We swapped vision for homesick depression. Voices that speak now about the future predict it will only get meaner and leaner, with success doled out to a precious few. And, by God, "the few" had better be us!

Is the past better than the future? Looking backward, we'll never know. Looking ahead, we need you to help us to strip pretense from a romanticized past when racism and sexism reigned and war was the quickest solution to joblessness. Help us to pick and choose, like browsers at an antique store, what was good enough *then* to bring into *now* as investments in our *future*. Be with us as we comfort ourselves with retrospectives and reruns.

Words of Light

"My people shall never again be dealt a blow like this. . . .
I will pour out my Spirit upon all of you! Your sons and daughters will prophesy; your old men will dream dreams, and your young men see visions." (Joel 2:27-28, TLB)

"I know that there is nothing better than for them to rejoice and to do good in one's lifetime . . . ." (Ecclesiastes 3:12 NASB)

"We confidently and joyfully look forward to actually becoming all that God has had in mind for us to be." (Romans 5:2, TLB)

Blindsided

The past is over and done. I've washed my hands of the whole matter. The past is past.

We are experts, O God, at going on, overcoming, being strong. We knew violent things happened, that we suffered, that we were affected. We looked at it, put it away. Then, boom, one day we were blindsided by flashbacks.

Flashbacks, Lord. An ominous word and a mixed blessing, at best. They leave us shaken, afraid. Reassure us that they are simply symptoms of things we put away until we felt safe enough to tell them, first to ourselves, then to you, and finally to caring others.

Whether we were in war zones, childhood bedrooms, parking lots, or our own pleasant living rooms, the enemy attacked. Whether with a single blow or a series of torments, the violence destroyed peace of mind, if nothing else. Our feelings about and from the attack are finally catching up with our words. Calm our jangling resistance. Send us strong, capable, tenacious companions for the journey back and forth.

Be with us when flashbacks—clues, really—ambush. Like Jesus' disciples in the boat, we are afraid of capsizing, running aground, getting hung up in a submerged tree. We hear his words, "Peace, be still." We recite them like a litany in sweaty, tempest-tossed moments. Help us to lance and tend wounds that have festered and throbbed below the surface for years.

Regardless of how dark and treacherous the future seems from this fragile vantage point, it is certainly better than the past. Reassure us that we are strong, wonderful, and recovering because we have courage enough to look back in order to go on.

Words of Light

You will not be afraid of the terror by night. . . . "I will be with him in trouble; I will rescue him. . . ." (Psalm 91:5,15, NASB)

Bravery

Like a flag waving above the parade of our reclaimed lives, God of David, who faced down a giant, we carry a banner of bravery. Multicolored like your favorite rainbows, our banner bears witness to many brave and courageous acts. We have learned that to be valiant and brave may mean . . .

. . . learning to fight back with fists, key rings, and fingernails.

. . . kicking feet and screaming, should a next time come.

. . . running as far and as fast as we can. (Brave is not foolish.)

. . . prosecuting and testifying, looking violators in the eye.

. . . setting our own pace for recovery, even if others think we should be done and be okay again.

. . . monitoring situations, people, places, and then getting the heck away.

And sometimes, O God, being brave also means . . .

. . . avoiding certain places, not doing certain things with certain people who might trigger memories and feelings we are not yet ready to explore;

. . . and _____ .

We know that as you guided the small shepherd boy David, you will lead us to find the right stones to use in our lives as we face the giants that stalk us in deed or thought. Thank you for helping us to feel brave again.

Words of Light

"Fear not, for I am with you, . . . I will strengthen you . . . ." (Isaiah 41:10, RSV)

Face to Face:
A Healing Moment

Bullies claimed victory over us the first time, but never again, God of strength. We are ready to take back what they stole: self-esteem. It is time to "de-myth" them. They never had the power they claimed. Remind us to be gentle with ourselves for believing it at first; it was an intense message they demanded we believe. We know now bullies have no real, lasting power.

Stand with us as we face them to say, *"I am learning to be okay again. Your hatefulness will not make me hate, especially not hate myself. Your misuse will not make me less than I am. Your evil will not block out my sun in an obscene eclipse."*

Whether we do this in unmailed letters to anonymous attackers or face to face in the family, give us courage. Steady us when a bully gets sympathy and exemption, while we get blame for being hard. "How can you?" we're challenged and pressed to recant. Remind us that we didn't start this, Lord, and that its aftermath doesn't belong to us.

Whisper, *"Give back shame that doesn't belong to you."* Guide us past revenge. Plant seeds of forgiveness for our sakes. Reminds us that bullies are to be pitied, and help them to change. (Thank you, God, that it's not our job to make it happen.)

Protect us from emotional blackmail by those who want to keep us quiet. Give us broad shoulders to bear their parting shots. They can't hit a moving target, and we're out of here, on our way, moving on, wasting no time waiting to be bullied again. Let's go, Lord. Let the bullies eat our dust.

Words of Light

If your brother sins, go and reprove him in private; . . . If he does not listen to you, take one or two more with you. . . . (Matthew 18:15,16, NASB)

Whoever does not receive you, nor heed your words, as you go out . . . , shake off the dust of your feet. (Matthew 10:14, NASB)

Memorial Service

It is too late, O God. We failed to protect: Violence took its ultimate toll, and we are dressed in mourning clothes.

Kneel with us to honor innocent victims of rampant evil.

Console us with reminders of how we tried to help. Give us proper penance if we didn't help, cowards that we can be.

Forgive our self-absorption and reluctance to get involved.

In the promise of your love, we name and hold up to you . . .

. . . family;

. . . friends;

. . . strangers who fell victim to random violence on street corners, on jogging paths, in their own homes, in Oklahoma;

. . . victims of massacres and political insanities, from the Holocaust and ethnic cleansings in faraway countries, to lynchings, mob bashings, and drive-by shootings.

Hold them on your home-coming lap like a mother does her children. Soothe away their last terror-filled memories. Steady us as we remember them, for their deaths must not be forgotten as easily as the headlines or sound bites that sum up their lives.

Show us what we can do to honor their lives—not their deaths. Hear and bless our pledge to them:

We stand at your graveside and promise that our grief will be active and forceful so you will not have lived and died in vain. We pledge to make our grief a living *and* doing *tribute to you. It will not fade and become a brittle imitation of the real thing, like plastic flowers in this cemetery, all shell and no life, no color. We will pray and work for justice and peace in your name.*

We pray, O God, that you will make our graveside litany a call to peace, not war, even a war on crime or violence, a war that has been tried and found flawed. Give us new language, new vision, and energy. Show us again, Lord of new beginnings even in death, a better way to live. We cannot continue this way; our loss is too great.

Words of Light

Love is strong as death . . . . (Song of Solomon 8:6, RSV)

Caution, Not Fear

"Oh, Mother dear, may we go for a swim?
Why, yes my darling children.
Just hang your clothes on a hickory limb
and don't go near the water." (Anonymous)

The fruit, O God, does not fall far from the tree: Kids are
as frightened by the fear they see in us as the fear they see
in reality! Ditto, friend and neighbor. We are making ourselves, our kids, and each other into fraidy-cats, as if we
were holding up warning signs that say "HALT: LIFE IS
DANGEROUS!"

Before we go any further, we pray now for our loved
ones' safety. We name them: _____.

We also pray for ourselves, for it is terrifying to let
mates and friends go on trips, to work, or shopping. It is
terrifying to let kids walk to school or get out of sight in a
mall. It is breath-stopping fearsome to send them off as
teens in cars, to campuses, and to jobs where violence has
easier access.

Some have decided it is safer to sit indoors (bring the
kids in, too) and watch television than to play outside.
That may well be true, but, O God, we cry in despair, what
kind of choice is this? We will, though, do whatever we can
to keep our loved ones safe from the epidemic of violence
spreading like the common cold that kids pick up on the
playgrounds we won't let them visit alone!

When is warning prophecy? When do warnings stunt
growth and strand us in fear? How can we protect our
loved ones, families, kids, friends, without becoming neu-
rotic?

What are we to do?

We can face our own fears and quit being so frightened
ourselves.

We hear this assurance and advice in your steadying voice as we reread your words, loving Parent. We know you would not send us into danger any more than we would send our young. Help us to get smart instead of scared. Inspire us to role play "Strangers" and "What to do if . . . ?" with our kids. Keep us open to kids' questions, revelations, concerns. Place your hand over our mouths to stifle horrified gasps and overreacting warnings when they tell us what has happened. Guide us to set up buddy-system phone calls and check-ins with friends, kin, neighbors— "You watch my back door, I'll watch yours" sorts of arrangements.

Remind us to trust our intuition, a great resource from you, and to pass on this skill to our kids so they, too, can become street smart. Prevent us from becoming dour hermits who peek from behind drapes at a world you intended for our enjoyment. Help us creatively to prepare kids with coping, not cowering skills.

Whew, we are exhausted, O God, from the effort of thinking about this approach. Renew our energy for actually doing it. We are grateful to know that through your guidance, fear need not have the last word when we tell bedtime stories to our children, and that we can balance fear and caution. Otherwise, it's "Everybody out of the water," and adults and kids alike are spectators instead of celebrants in the great splashing, sun-dappled swim of life.

Words of Light

Let him have all your worries and cares, for he is always thinking about you and watching everything that concerns you. (1 Peter 5:7, TLB)

Sorrow into Joy

Is it okay to be okay? How in heaven's name can we know? Violation—old or fresh—has banished us so far from joy that we doubt we can find our way—*if* we deserve joy. Experts call this "survivor guilt." We call it chronic pain; it defines our days.

We can't sleep without disturbed dreams, much less smile when awake. *Joy* is a detergent and *Pride* a polish. *Play* is what others do. Help us to claim them for ourselves. Help us to understand that being "okay" is not the absence of sadness, and "going on" is not the absence of grief, especially if it's familiar violators of family, friend we must leave behind. To the contrary, God of healed hearts, to mourn is to be different from violators: They are the ones who feel nothing. Thank God for sorrow, we whisper in our nighttime prayers.

But enough is enough. Give us more than sorrow. Give us joy and delight. Is it too late? We hear your resounding chuckle, "Of course not. Let children come to me." No matter how grey our hair and how long ago the trauma, help us to retrieve childlike trust, wonder, and joy, and to play like children at your knee, knowing that we are the apples of your eye.

It's hard to play with hands clenched into fists that are ready for self-defense. Open them now while we're standing close to you. Let the pain we've hoarded fall like birdseed on snow to swell in the rain of spring tears and to grow ripe with joy in the summer. Winter is past.

Words of Light

The winter is past, the rain is over and gone. The flowers appear on the earth. (Song of Solomon 2:11-12, RSV)

We confidently and joyfully look forward to actually becoming all that God has had in mind for us to be." (Romans 5:2, TLB)

Keep me as the apple of your eye. (Psalm 17:8, NIV)

Personal Restoration

Eeny, Meeny, Miny

There are sixteen violent stories in today's paper, Lord—on just two pages. Words like *hatred, bitter, slay, slap, dismantle, anti, target, squash, destroy, bomb, murdered, fume, accuse* tell the tales of why we should give up hoping that we will be able to live nonviolently. I could name you a dozen, fifty, a hundred more reasons why we'd be justified.

Yet, like a speed bump in the drive-through, you have placed a decision in the path, reminding us that hope is a choice. Teach us that choosing to live as people of hope is not to diminish or belittle pain and suffering or to lie about evil's reality. Rather, it is, O God, simply to cling to your promise to make all things new.

We find renewal in small things: a smile from a stranger, negotiation and compromise in just one conflict, talking face to face, airing differences. Are these too small to keep us hankering after hope? No, for the cycles of destruction are interrupted . . . again and again. . . . We find ourselves surprised by joy, moved by others, and reaching beyond defensiveness and mistrust to love.

When we get too impatient and discouraged, remind us that the Hebrew word for *hope* means "to twist or twine" and is related to *kiven* for spiderweb. So much of our hoping has this quality, the quality of incredible strength that first appears as fragile, insignificant strands. Think how far it takes the spider, how it supports life. Bless our tiny-strand hope, O God, and help us to twist it into sturdy ropes of commitment to peace.

Words of Light

Try to live in peace even if you must run after it to catch and hold it! (1 Peter 3:11, TLB)

"I have set before you life and death, blessing and curse; therefore choose life . . . ." (Deuteronomy 30:19, RSV)

Across the Sands of Time

Upset, the kids found the hermit crab dead in our aquarium today. But as I plucked his lifeless body out of the water, antennae waved from a large shell on the "ocean" floor: It was our hermit. I was holding just his shed skin. Crabs, we learned, must continually move into larger shells to accommodate growth or be suffocated, even though it takes time to fill up the new shell. We plasticized his shed skin as a paperweight, a reminder of Mother Nature's wise provision. Journal entry, 1974

Life was so simple before violence struck. Now it's broken pieces and shattered illusions. We hunker down to inspect and repair them behind a wall of fear, fortified with an arsenal of cynicism and plans for retaliation. This is a cozy place we've made for ourselves, Lord. Come on in.

Is it your spirit making us feel crowded? so out of air that we must huff and puff even to breathe in our cramped quarters? Is it you beckoning us to come out of hiding and to begin the journey to healing?

Go away, go away, go away.

O dear God, we wail, don't make us move. Don't ask us to change and venture from this haven of suffering. We've wounds to tend, scores to settle, dangers to avoid. *Go away, go away.* Is it you who is making us curious about why we should come out? why we should move on? We're getting along okay. Is it you holding up a mirror to show us just how uncomfortable we really are in our cozy exile? We are angry that you won't leave us to our misery.

Yet, if we look around we'll understand: Even hermit crabs know to trust your nudging. They must change shells or be suffocated. Don't we want to grow? to become more the people you created us to be—before violence brought us to a standstill? Help us to not fight the natural tendency to heal, to grow, to go on.

Dear crab, you do naturally what we fight: change. But Lord, we protest, a crab clad only in new skin when it briefly leaves a too-large new shell to seek algae is vulnerable to sea creatures. There may be "sea creatures" after us. But do we want to be as immobile as paperweights? Do we want to remain hostage to sea creatures? We add our questions to the stuff we've accumulated in our hideout.

Give us courage to explore beyond this place of pain, denial, anger—whatever it is that keeps us stuffed into places we no longer fit. The anxiety we feel may be from running out of breathing room. Hold out a hand; we're emerging to breathe deeply, stretch, stand tall, move freely.

Words of Light

Lay aside the old self . . . and be renewed in the spirit of your mind . . . and put on the new self . . . in the likeness of God . . . . (Ephesians 4:22-24, NASB)

Potpourri

6 ounces rose petals
1 oz. each lemon verbena leaves, crumbled bay leaves,
dried orange peel, orris root
2 drops each rose oil and lemon oil
6-inch cinnamon stick, crushed
Mix petals, leaves and dry spices. Add oils a drop at a
time, mixing well.
Seal in a plastic bag for six weeks, shaking every other day.

We bulldozed a scrap of riverbank and built a house, O God, with you as the cornerstone. The yard was insistently derelict, as I worry our world is, despite efforts to tame it. As weeds overtake a garden, so greed, power-lust, and self-absorption produce frenzied fringes and murderous children. Sad, I seek you outdoors, where you seem to mock my gardening efforts with a stubborn, lanky tendril I'm unable to snip, clip, or pull out.

Are we, "lanky tendrils" of peacemakers, all you have for changing your world? We feel woefully inadequate, fearing that we lanky, straggly ones have little chance of outlasting uncaring, for-the-hell-of-it bullies who uproot lives. O God, be realistic.

You are, I realize, astonished: My garden's lanky tendril is blooming. It is a rose planted decades ago! A bulldozer couldn't dislodge it; my clippers couldn't thwart it. It blooms in chaos, reminding me that you are a powerful resource, redeeming the effects of violence, securing healing for violated bodies and souls, strengthening us for living free from fear, and, yes, even making peace happen. *Lanky* and *straggly* are other words for resilient!

I felt your hand on mine, Creator God, when, racing to beat an early frost, I collected rose blooms. They, like our days, no matter how chaotic, can be blended by your hand into a potpourri of enduring possibilities.

Words of Light

God works for good with those who love him. (Romans 8:28, RSV)

Why Aren't We Spared?

For God's sake, where are you when we are violated? Why do you let meanness, violation happen? What do you gain from our suffering? Are you testing loyalty? evaluating the breadth and width of our faith?

What, designer, sustainer, and operator of creation, is your purpose in letting evil overgrow faith like poison ivy in a rose garden?

Is violation your will?

We need answers. If you are going to help us to recover, we can't believe you would send violence, let it happen, watch, evaluate our responses, and turn coldly away. You cannot dispense violation and healing at the same time and still be a God we trust to heal. You cannot have it both ways; you cannot be a double-minded, two-faced parent. What, O God, are we to do with you?

We hear you weep with us, hear you groan in frustration when we again do what we're told not to for our own good, when some of us choose evil. Yet we will feel your healing touch if we stumble into that path.

Evil and its fallout, violence, is not about you; it is about us. From the first of time, we persisted in eating forbidden fruits. Our willful disobedience, not your intention, loving Parent, brings us violence, pain. It is the randomness of a free-will world, not your hand selecting and putting them to torturous test, that snares the innocent.

No violations are your will; no suffering, your design. You intend wholeness and peace for all. As we hunker down beneath degrading, terrifying violation—big or small, premeditated or random, old or fresh—we feel your loving hand. We recall how close you stayed to your Son, who talked to you about this will business even from the cross. Like him, we know you are near us in the chaos of a mortal world. Your tears overflow ours.

In that assurance, forgive our hasty blame of you. Forgive us for considering even for a moment that any parent would willfully harm one of his or her own children. (What would you have to gain?)

Guide us in the convoluted paths of a free-will life where, no longer alone in the exile we made for ourselves, we mend. Your energy will restore us to abundant life, your original intention for your children.

Words of Light

"Which one of you, if his son asks for . . . a fish, will give him a snake? . . . How much more will your Father in heaven give good gifts to those who ask him!" (Matthew 7:9-11, NIV)

"I came that they may have life, and have it abundantly." (John 10:10, RSV)

"Men loved the darkness rather than the light." (John 3:19, NASB)

A Mustard-Flavored Harvest

Fields of mustard plants unfold across the Scottish countryside in golden promise. We take heart, God of gardens and fields, in their vast sprawl, for they sprout from tiniest seed.

Can we in these days of harsh words and eroding spirit find enough mustard seeds of change to sow? Think what a harvest it would be if we all took a few tiny nubbins and planted and tended them as well as we do fear!

Read with us between the lines of clever, wise books to find the powerful truth about small, random acts of kindness. They tell of the ground swell of energy that can make a difference. Think of the first disciples, followers, the early church, whose catacomb faith houses us today. Make our imaginations fertile plots where new ideas for our own acts of goodness can sprout. Guide our hands to make a list of three very, very small things to do just this week:

1.

2.

3.

We must believe small deeds matter, O God, for you say mountains can be moved cross country with faith this small. We don't always see it, for foolishly we wait for cosmic thunderbolts and overlook flickers of goodness that swirl around us like firefly messages begging to be noticed and gathered into a radiant harvest of hope. We will add our three things, three tiny things, to the crop. Bless and multiply it a thousandfold.

Words of Light

"If you had faith even as small as a tiny mustard seed you could say to this mountain, 'Move!' and it would go far away. Nothing would be impossible." (Matthew 17:20, TLB)

Stand Up and Be Counted

A tough question for you, wise God: Should we turn away or confront when we encounter hate messages on shirt, bumper sticker, electronic communique, church sign, political poster, commercial? when we hear obscenities in music? when we witness mob frenzy pretending to be holy cause? when we find bigotry masquerading as humor, rape as fun? The list goes on and on, but the question remains on our lips.

If we confront, we risk; if we ignore, we condone. Too many tough questions these days.

Help us to find answers. We need to stand up against haters who say they—as citizen, faithful, patriot—speak for us. Give us courage to name their deceit. Gird us with vision for a better world that starts with the first step—our rising to our feet. Simplistic as it may sound, O God, that's where we must begin; turnarounds happen in our backyard first or not at all. Forgive our lack of trust in you when we wait for global transformation that doesn't require anything, especially confronting bullies, from us!

We're ready to stand with you to find new ways to solve old problems that begin with powerful versus powerless, haves against have-nots.

In the settling dust of a heartland bombing, a call to peace rings out. Inspire us to stand and be counted with those who are for peace, negotiation, tolerance, dialogue, respect, protecting all people. In the long run, that's the only way we can come close to protecting ourselves.

Stand with us to be counted on the side of peace.

Words of Light

Do not let what is for you a good thing be spoken of as evil; . . . Let us pursue the things which make for peace and the building up of one another. (Romans 14:16-19 NASB)

". . . do not merely look out for your own personal interests, but for the interests of others . . . ." (Philippians 2:1-4, NASB)

In Our Honor

Take our hands in yours, dear God, and clap them together. *Clap, clap, clap,* until it sounds like applause.

We need you to teach us how to applaud for ourselves so we can honor ourselves for coping during the violence done to us. We did well. Lead us in reciting that over and over. *We did well, we did well, we did well.*

We sometimes worry that we should have acted differently. We worry that we gave in, colluded, participated, invited, encouraged the violation. But we didn't, O God, we didn't. Help us to know and believe this.

Help us to understand that when we were in the midst of terror, we did what we believed was best. What we did brought us to now, a triumph if ever there was one. We traveled by the light we had at the time. *Applause, applause.*

Hindsight is 20/20, and now as adults some of us too quickly say, when looking back to childhood violation, "I would never allow that" or "I'd call the police." But we were children then. Help us to remember that as children we did our best *as* children. *Applause, applause.*

On this side of violations in the adult world, some of us second-guess what we should've done. But we were cornered then. Help us to remember that when people held knives at our throats and evil squeezed us in its grasp, we did what we had to do to survive. *Applause, applause.*

Help us to honor whatever we did wherever and whenever we were misused. Stand and cheer with us, O God, as we applaud our clever acts of survival, inspired by your indwelling spirit. We are ready to take a curtain call at the threshold of the rest of life, built as it is upon our amazing survival.

Applause, applause.

Words of Light

"You were tired out by the length of your road, Yet you did not say, 'It is hopeless.' You found renewed strength, Therefore you did not faint." (Isaiah 57:10, NASB)

Battle Ribbons

On down the road after violence against us, God of amazing victories, we want to be veterans of violence rather than its victims or survivors. Veterans wear battle ribbons and use firsthand knowledge to help them to go on, while survivors stay linked to the battle, and victims forever repeat it. We know: Been there, done that.

Help us to transcend the hellish past that brings nightmares and flashbacks. Give us courage to view it and then to leave it behind. Help us to see ourselves as valiant, brave, resourceful for having survived.

I name my particular battlefield to you:
I encountered these enemies:
Heal the wounds they inflicted:
Bless the scars they left, my battle ribbons of victory:

Help us to heal by retelling our stories and replaying the scenes until they become no more and no less than a part of the past, like a scar on a shoulder. Veterans keep memories and mementos in a scrapbook on a shelf; we put ours there now, too. If we need to look at it again, turn its pages with us, O God, reminding us how brave we are, how far we've come since we lived in the battle zones. Then, like on other memorial days, let's go on a picnic and watch a parade; it's being thrown in our honor.

Words of Light

In all these things we are more than conquerors. (Romans 8:37, RSV)

To Dance Again

O dear God, how we want to dance! Like a character in an Elie Wiesel book, we say in the face of violence, "I will dance anyway" (*Gates of the Forest*), despite all that has gone on in our lives. But we don't know the dance steps, and one leg feels like it is shorter than the other.

Must violence forever limit us, making us limp a little in the happiness department? Must we succumb to depression and slink away from joy? We hear your resounding assurance that resurrection is not only possible, it comes daily. Raise us into lives of joy, to dance where we belong.

Find us where we, like wallflowers, are watching others dance, envying their carefree movement. Help us to understand that many of these dancers we so admire have been touched by violence—but that they have relearned the dance steps. They are pacesetters, pathfinders, we can follow.

Now that we have journeyed so far, if we agree with abusers who say we don't deserve better and thus choose to sit on the outside of life, the dance, we become victims again, this time by our own hands. But, O God, we do deserve better.

Pull us to our feet; gently nudge us onto the dance floor of life with them; and tap out a sprightly beat to get us moving. Remind us that our strength is your joy. Play the music louder as we accept our places among the grace-full dancers.

Words of Light

"The joy of the Lord is your strength. You must not be dejected and sad!" (Nehemiah 8:10, TLB)

Their life shall be like a watered garden, and all their sorrows be gone. The young girls will dance for joy, and menfolk—old and young—will take their part in all the fun; . . . . (Jeremiah 31:12-14, TLB)

A time to weep, and a time to laugh. (Ecclesiastes 3:4, NASB)

Can't Forgive a Monster

We've made violators into monsters that loom larger than life, immense, superhuman, like shadows cast on the wall. How can we forgive monsters that tower over us?

Shrink 'em to the proper size.

You, O God, are amazing. (We thank you for sharing your common-sense wisdom with us in these knee-shaking moments.) Monsters are not monsters at all. They just want us to think they are. Remind us that a new, monster-shrinking perspective does not ever, ever reduce the power of the evil they do or the enormous pain they cause. Rather, it reduces *the monsters themselves* to the boring, self-absorbed misfits they are.

Misfits, we can forgive. Misfits are not worth clinging to in past pain that we want to be rid of. Help us to forgive them, even though forgiving still feels a little like letting them go free. Help us to understand that it's the other way round: We are letting *us* go free.

To cower, unforgiving, in their grotesque shadows is to support their visions of themselves—that they are bigger than accountability, bigger than forgiveness. If we're so afraid of them that we can't forgive, we hand them the power they crave.

Remember "Shrinky Dinks"—plastic that could be painted and cut into charms and decorations? You put them in the oven big, and they came out tiny. Steady our hands, O God, as we put images of our monsters in the red-hot oven of rage and justice, and then let forgiveness shrink them back to boring size. Then it will be clear—it's not worth spending our lives fearing these puny folks.

Words of Light

Bless those who persecute you; . . . Leave room for God's wrath, . . . Overcome evil with good. (Romans 12:14-21, NIV)

Squandered Sorrow

What are we to do with the sorrow dumped on us like rancid trash? Unwanted and overwhelming, it is the leavings of violence against us. Yet, if we bury sorrow, like gold and talents in a field, it remains useless and incapable of becoming something with value for our lives.

But, O God, how can we be good stewards of unwanted sorrow? Is there stewardship—a right use—of the sorrow left from what happened to us? Guide us. We are at a crossroads, unsure of what to make from this sorrow: hate, bitterness, and fear? or redemption, strength?

Using our sorrow to hate keeps us stuck to the violators like burrs on a sock. Redemption, however, lets us treat our sorrow like frequent flyer miles: We can redeem it for something we want. (It's useless until we do.) Can we steward our sorrow by changing the way we use it? Help us to pick out what we'd rather have.

Show us those who already chose, creating good from bad, useful from useless—the mother who started MADD after her daughter was killed by a drunk driver; founders of victim support and advocacy groups; writers who share words of inspiration after witnessing murder, experiencing torture or kidnapping; stewards of sorrow.

Inspire us to look at sorrow the way the pioneers viewed the stones that littered the ground—as assets to be turned into walls, bridges, foundations; the way Solomon viewed his useless clay grounds—as a place to cast bronze vessels for the Lord's house. Teach us that sorrow ultimately can nourish us and others when we dig it up, assess it, and swap it for something of value.

Help us, Lord of vineyards and rolled-away stones, to be stewards, not hoarders, of sorrow. Lead us from storehouses of pain into marketplaces of hope. Inspire us to become savvy, wounded healers who know the value of our sorrow, trading it in for compassion and swapping pain for action.

Words of Light

All these vessels in the house of the LORD . . . were of burnished bronze. [King Solomon] cast them . . . in the clay grounds between Succoth and Zarethan. (1 Kings 7:45-46, RSV)

Hazardous Duty

We can't speak of violence, God of doves, without at least bringing up peace. We whisper when we speak of peace, for it is a volatile topic, and supporting it can be inflammatory. Your Son learned firsthand how dangerous it is for peacemakers. So, too, did Martin Luther King Jr., Mary the mother of Jesus, Abe Lincoln, and ____. The reading of the roster drones on and on; theirs is not a club we are eager to join. Turning the other cheek is unsafe, and praying for enemies is often called treachery.

If we don't kill "peaceniks," we ridicule them—"wimp," "chicken." Savvy to the ways of the world, we won't put ourselves at risk by advocating peaceful solutions to family fights or global conflagrations. It's easy to understand how Palm Sunday triumph became Good Friday murder.

Are we complicit in Good Friday? in its repeats? Forgive us, for some of us have a great deal invested in keeping hate alive. How cost-effective is peace? How marketable is cooperation? We use hate mongering to sell consumable goods, entertainment, news, and ways of life! Would we lose too much personal power if there were no battles? no enemies to posture against when we seek fame and spoils? We confess there is profit in trouble and power in winning. That we might prefer battle to peace for self-serving reasons is a sobering possibility. Give us the courage to face our motivations. Remind us that both peace and violence are results of our choices. Give us the courage to choose peace, for you will be there working for peace with us. You are the still, small voice that keeps us going back again and again to the bargaining table when a bomb would settle it once and for all. Inspire us to teach peace, not war, to children. Forgive us when we create conditions that spawn violators, killers, bombers—the peace killers. Encourage us, O God, to reread the verse about peace: It says "peace *within* you," not "peace *with* you." Help us to make room for peace in our inner arsenals, already loaded with defenses and anger. Forgive our lazy approach to peace, as if it were some *thing* we acquire and hold, rather than something that holds us.

No question, peace is foolhardy and dangerous. It is also the only game in town in which we can all wind up victors, because peace is not about winning and losing; it is about surviving. It begins when I hold out my hand and stick out my neck in peace-possible ways. Protect our backsides, Watcher of the night, against snipers who want to shoot out the lights we carry to the peace table.

Shalom.

Words of Light

I will now say, "May peace be within you." (Psalm 122:8, NASB)

Thanks-living

We made it, God of Red Sea escapes and dream warnings, to this far side of violation. We recognize, are grateful for, your companionship in:

• Healers, interveners, advocates who believed and led
I am grateful.

•The gift of forgetting until we are strong enough to remember
I am grateful.

• The gift of remembering just a little bit at a time
I am grateful.

• Dreams . . . and pen and voice . . . to record clues for healing
I am grateful.

• Pens and pencils, to doodle and draw anew on the canvas of stolen innocence—whether we were adult or child at the moment of violation; and paints, to color that pain until it bleeds off the edges of that canvas and away from daily life
I am grateful.

• Stories, poetry, songs, letters, notes that tell our truths between the lines
I am grateful.

• Tears that wash away toxins and nourish seedling hope
I am grateful.

• The marvelous ways we stayed alive
I am grateful.

• A day without thinking of the violation, reliving the terror and helplessness
I am grateful.

• Babies who link us to the past and the future, while insisting that we live in the present
I am grateful.

- Partners', mates', families', and friends' bewildered, believing support

I am grateful.

- Symptoms, the lifesavers that got our attention

I am grateful.

-

(Write about a way God has been your companion.)
I am grateful.

-

I am grateful.

- Nagging, nudging pressure to move toward light when we prefer dark

I am grateful.

- Laughing again; dancing through fall leaves, spring showers, snowflakes

I am grateful.

- Curiosity about tomorrow, the day after, next month, next year

I am grateful.

- A desire to reconnect with others, to be a resource, to share, to pass on healing

I am grateful.

Words of Light

For thou hast been my help, And in the shadow of thy wings I sing for joy. (Psalm 63:7, NASB)

Unhooked

Thomas Edison said, after repeated failures to invent the light bulb, that because of his failures, he knew what a light bulb isn't. We know what forgiveness isn't. We've tried it all, O God. It isn't forgetting what others did, although memory seems to be fading. It isn't overlooking, tolerating. It isn't excusing, exempting. It isn't covering up for people we need to set free to live their consequences. It isn't trivializing vileness and monstrous obscenities or diminishing the pain. It isn't premature, cheap lip service.

At long last, we discover forgiveness is a gift from you.

In a slow, fits-and-starts process, forgiveness heals hurts we never deserved. By forgiving violators, we are forgiving you for creating a mortal, free-will world. In that world, when we search, we find not answers, but rather a Presence, which we need more than answers. We are also learning to forgive ourselves for being unforgiving! Together, dear God, we have come a long way. Feel us stretch tall and limber, now that we've laid down our burdens of bitterness. Look through our eyes at a new world resurrected from pain that should never have been. Run your hands with ours over scarred wounds that no longer fester.

We are grateful for the wisdom of forgiveness in an Aztec ritual: The shaman "plucks" a fish hook from the neck of a person who has not been able to forgive. "Now you are free," the shaman says, showing the hook. Hidden between his fingers, the hook has left a small nick to bleed away toxins and to heal. Today we reach up a hand and feel blood and the imprint of a hook removed from our souls.

Now we, too, can be free of self-imposed misery.

Words of Light

Thou art a God of forgiveness, Gracious and compassionate . . . (Nehemiah 9:17, NASB)